Cheering For Self

Cheering For Self

An Ethnography of the Basketball Event

James S. Vass, Jr.

iUniverse, Inc.
New York Lincoln Shanghai

Cheering For Self
An Ethnography of the Basketball Event

All Rights Reserved © 2003 by James S. Vass, Jr.

No part of this book may be reproduced or transmitted in any form or by any means, graphic, electronic, or mechanical, including photocopying, recording, taping, or by any information storage retrieval system, without the written permission of the publisher.

iUniverse, Inc.

For information address:
iUniverse
2021 Pine Lake Road, Suite 100
Lincoln, NE 68512
www.iuniverse.com

ISBN: 0-595-27980-5

Printed in the United States of America

Contents

Preface vii
    Current Season's Success vii
    Notes For Preface x

Cheering for Self: An Ethnography of the basketball event 1
    New Role as an Ethnographer and Analyst 1
    'Basketball event' defined 2
    Imagined Communities 3
    UW Basketball History 7
    My Basketball Experience 8
    Structure of this Thesis 9
    Notes for Chapter One 10

A Narrative Script of the Basketball Event 12
    The Conclusion Briefly Stated 12
    Geography of the Arena 12
    'The Basketball Event'6 17
    Pre-Game 17
    First-Half 20
    Halftime 22
    Second Half 23
    Post-Game 26
    Practice 27
    Some Identified Patterns 29
    Notes for Chapter Two 35

An Interpretation and Analysis of the Key Patterns .38
    Concepts1 38
    A Brief Narrative Structure or Sequence of the Basketball Event 40
    Cheering for Self Explained 41
    Loudness Levels 42
    Relative Loudness Levels or hierarchy of Event Moments 42
    Advertising: Ads are Everywhere to be Seen, Heard, and Experienced 45
    Notes for Chapter Three 49

Appendix 1: Ticket Brochures and Schedule 53

Appendix 2: List of Logos, Words,
and Phrases observed at Basketball Events 55

Reference Bibliography 59

References 63

Index 143

Preface

This paper is a study of UW men's basketball fans during the 2001-2002 season and explores their proclivity to 'cheering for self' during basketball events. An undercurrent runs throughout this participant observation mini-ethnography dealing with access, and the relative quality of that access, to 'basketball events' being affected by ones age, class, race, and gender. The prominent role of advertising in shaping basketball events and helping to construct fans as consumers of products (both commercial and institutional) during the process of 'cheering for self' is central to this thesis.

Current Season's Success

At this writing the University of Wyoming (UW) Cowboys are having an excellent season. UW has an at-large bid to play in the men's National Collegiate Athletic Association (NCAA) post-season tournament for the first time in over a decade.[1]

Last season ended with a last second loss in the first round of the National Invitation Tournament (NIT) to Pepperdine. During the off-season the Wyoming Cowboys recruited and signed one of the top high school point guards in the nation and also a former junior college high scoring guard. Both became starters during their first year on the team despite the team's pre-existing high level of talent. Two other transfer players, including a six foot-eleven-inch center, were signed. Those two must sit out one year before playing but can practice with the team. One player left the team citing a lack of playing time.

The consensus among fans is that Wyoming lacked good perimeter shooting last year (i.e. outside the 3-point arc), but now the team has new starting guards that get the job done. Although Wyoming could go far in the NCAA tournament the team still lacks a superstar center over seven feet tall.

This year the team has worked on defense, supplementing a prolific offense and is one of the top teams in the nation in out-rebounding opponents. Each season the team has won at least one more game than the previous season, beginning with eighteen wins in 1999 and finishing with twenty-two wins this year. The coach's compensation package consists of an elaborate contract worth over five hundred thousand dollars per year over the next seven years, provided incentive conditions are met, including certain attendance levels by fans.

One current player is a Wyoming native, making this team especially popular. A quadruple overtime win during this season was the longest game in Wyoming basketball history and is a defining moment for this season. On February 4, 2002, the Cowboys defeated the Utah Utes[2], thereby ending the longest NCAA basketball home winning streak in the nation. The Wyoming Cowboys won their regular season before the largest crowd ever to attend a game in the Arena Auditorium (AA)—or "double A", and then drew thousands of fans to Las Vegas for the Mountain West Conference (MWC) post-season tournament and to Albuquerque for the NCAA post-season tournament.

In the first round of the 2002 NCAA tournament UW will play and beat Gonzaga University, a team with a 29-3 record that was rated sixth in the nation by the Associated Press Poll. The opponent's star player, Dan Dickau, was selected a first string All-America by the Associated Press. UW then played in the second round of the NCAA Tournament against 7th ranked Arizona (a regional #3 seed and team that played in last year's title game) and the son (Luke Walton) of a former NBA star player for the Portland Trailblazers—Bill Walton.

Expectations are high for the future of UW basketball, and for publicity for the university. Fans and the University of Wyoming President are not ruling out another NCAA Basketball Championship for the Wyoming Cowboys sometime during the current coach's era. There is the expectation that success in the basketball program within the athletic department will help to increase the enrollment at the University of Wyoming.

Despite the team's remarkable success this year, the nature of the basketball event has not been different in essence from other years. Though the individual participants in the 'basketball event' change, its basic nature is remarkably stable. If one compares the present to five, ten, or even twenty years in the past, the experience of the fan changes little. Only the individual actors in the 'basketball events' (i.e. coach, players, and students) change. The power of an institution within an institution to resist change and live on is demonstrated by the basketball event. The present season has created hyper-fandom. Increased fan levels have attracted more advertising. The addition of video screens large enough for all in the AA to see has helped to spawn the addition of new traditions, many of which will be discussed later in this thesis: "kiss cam" that focuses on couples in the stands, video clip ads, video film clips as time fillers and to get the crowd pumped up, video replays like one might see on TV, video of the U.S. flag during the National Anthem, video of UW fund raising projects like the new Veteran's Memorial to be constructed at the football stadium, displaying Cotton-eyed Joe, zooming in on cheerleaders and the wildfire dance troupe, etc. In effect the large video screen makes the basketball event mirror that of watching pro football at home but of course along with the live experience.

This study explores fan landscape, or fanscape, during University of Wyoming basketball games. Through a participant observation mini-ethnography of the basketball event, I establish its narrative sequence and hierarchy, both scripted and collective.

What are the traditions, and imagined communities in the basketball event and where are the characters located culturally and spatially? Just exactly what is going on during a 'basketball event' as a result of history and future expectations in this institution within an institution? Analysis and critical interpretation based on participant observation of the 'basketball event' lead to a discovery of its defining moments and an overriding theme. The view that fans are 'cheering for themselves' seems to be reflected in fan behavior and helps explain why many fans take the games so personally. 'Cheering for self' is the activity engaged in by individual fans after they find things to identify or connect with through personal investment.

One final interesting note: at an altitude of over seven thousand feet, the University of Wyoming has the highest Division I basketball court in the nation. This fact adds distinction to basketball events that occur in Laramie, Wyoming. Because of the altitude, many teams refuse to play in Laramie, fearing that a fast paced game will tire their team out and result in a loss. Whether or not this is true, the sign, "Welcome to 7220 feet," is an important part of this environment.

Notes For Preface

[1] UW wins in the first round over the 6th ranked team in the nation but falls in a close game in the second round to a 7th ranked team. After the season was over one of UW's assistant coaches accepted a head coach position at another school. He also took another UW coach with him to fill the roll of an assistant with more responsibility than he had before. UW signed one of the top players out of Colorado and another Nigerian from a community college that has produced NBA players in the past to play next season. One UW player who has another year of eligibility is trying out for the NBA but may end up coming back to UW for one more year. It is believed that UW will be listed in top 25 polls next year.

[2] Carol Spindel in her book *Dancing at Halftime: Sports and the Controversy over American Indian Mascots* explains why sport mascot's portraying Native Americans (e.g. the Utah Utes and the San Diego Aztec's) bothers some Native Americans. Chief Illiniwek is the sport mascot for the Illinois basketball team.

> Another day, as I sat in Wendy's eating hamburgers with my son, I pointed out the chief wallpaper next to our table. "I've heard that some Native American people don't like the idea of Chief Illiniwek," I told him.
>
> "Yeah," my son said casually. "Like if David dressed up in my clothes and pretended to be me at school and then did something really stupid on the playground." As if the matter were settled, he returned to dragging his French fries through little ponds of ketchup to coat them, first on one side, then on the other. (Spindel, 2000, p. 4)

Utah Utes may be offensive to Native Americans while, as discussed more fully later, BYU is found to be offensive to some UW students.

Chapter One:

Cheering for Self: An Ethnography of the Basketball Event

> The only obligation which I have a right to assume, is to do at any time what I think right.
>
> Henry David Thoreau, *Civil Disobedience*, 1849
> (Thoreau, 1849, p. 2)

Fortuitously, the season I chose in which to study the UW men's basketball team was a championship season and arguably one of the best years in Wyoming history for fans. This made studying of fan behaviors especially interesting, as the fan base grew to support regular as well as outlier behaviors—like that of rabid fans.

New Role as an Ethnographer and Analyst

To collect observations of the 'basketball event' for analysis and support of the 'cheering for self' hypothesis there needs to be a framework or device allowing consistency and thoroughness. A discussion of the chosen mode follows.

Camille Bacon-Smith's book, *Enterprising Women: Television Fandom and the Creation of Popular Myth*, provides a useful model for my examination of UW basketball fan behavior. Her discussion about methodology, ethnography, hierarchy, community, visual meaning, identity and narrative provide insight to approaching this participant mini-ethnography of fans and the 'basketball event.'

Ethnography is a data-intensive method in which the researcher studies the culture of informants where they gather in their own native habitats...[to form a] structure and meaning of the fan language...If you want to know what something means in a culture, ask. But to understand the answer, you have to speak the language—the special symbolic dialect—of the community, the audience you wish to study. (Bacon-Smith, 1992, p. 299)

This means that one has to become a fan in order to study and write about fans using this technique. I did not become a rabid fan, but during the season I became an extremely loyal, and dedicated fan of the 'basketball event.' Some non-fans do not even know a 'basketball event' is occurring, though some fans may drive or fly hundreds of miles to experience one.

I have become a fan of UW's Coach Steve McClain. The basketball event is more meaningful because he seems to have the team headed in the right direction. Watching him during a few games in past seasons and most of the home games this season reveals the uniqueness of this UW coach's style. His way of coaching, unlike any I have seen at UW or anywhere else, leads one to believe that it is just a matter of time until he takes UW to the final four.

While quotations of academic texts are liberally utilized in this paper, most observations and comments on observations are readily apparent to anyone attending 'basketball events.' Material drawn from field notes on the 'basketball event' are not backed up with citations or verified across multiple basketball seasons. By limiting the use of actual names and generalizing somewhat, this thesis should be more accessible for future readers.[1]

This Thesis, unlike any of the studies of basketball discussed in a note (p. 115) looks at the 'basketball event' from the perspective of a fan. No characters on the "stage" of the 'basketball event' (that is, involved in the play of the game itself) were interviewed. Discussion occurred with some non-fans and those that attended the 'basketball event' with me.

'Basketball event' defined

The term 'basketball event' is used rather than 'basketball game' to make clear that everything connected to and seen, heard, or experienced before, during, and after a basketball game is included. The actual game itself is only part of the 'basketball event.'

My methodology for completing this ethnography was as follows. I attended fan events that are part of the basketball event like any other fan, while observing and taking notes. My notes were often brief shorthand. After the basketball event, I typed up my observations and filled in the blanks, adding new things that I recalled, and reflecting on my experience and my feelings. The next day, I reflected on my observations. Finally my observations were consolidated into a field notes journal of my participant observation mini-ethnography.

When a fan jumps up and yells out, what does this mean? Is the fan happy or mad? What caused the fan to yell? What is the fan trying to communicate and what do other fans think the fan is trying to communicate? [2]

Identifying patterns, interpreting, and analyzing are the next steps in the approach taken in this study. My gaze has been shaped by American Studies. Having learned to question what I see and to notice hegemonic realities, as well as to note minutiae and abstract binary oppositions provides new insight to old visions. No longer blind to some ideas and conscious of ideology, I experience events differently. A seemingly simple basketball game has become a complex experience.

As Eric Sandeen explains in his book *Picturing an Exhibition: The Family of Man and 1950's America*:

> Culture is a "screen or filter" that brings certain phenomena or qualities of the environment to this personality or blocks some stimuli from reaching it, thereby accounting for a dynamic national character that is reflected in individuals who exhibit its traits differently. (Sandeen, 1995, p. 6)

My observations are an attempt to shake loose from constructed and learned impressions and to notice not what I think is there during basketball games but rather what really is going on during the basketball event.

Imagined Communities

UW basketball fans are connected to each other through the basketball event. This community of fans is more abstract than real. An imagined community is one that is abstract, existing only in the mind. Examples include nations, political parties, and institutions. These imagined communities have great power in bringing the current meaning of a word like 'fan' closer to its original meaning—of 'fanatic.'[3]

Attending University of Wyoming basketball games, autograph sessions, and open practices to observe fan behavior, fan gaze, and event voices provided various views of fans. Fan gaze is not only where fans focus their eyes but also why they chose to look there and what they are thinking before during and after looking. I also watched games on television and listened to them on the radio. I also gathered some information via ticket brochures, media guides, sports news on TV & the coach's TV show on Sundays, the university athletics web site which includes archived audio of games, 6th Man Club, national ranking polls, sports talk shows on radio, open practices in the Arena Auditorium; newspapers, books, and journals. Other informants attended the basketball event with me, including some non-fans, providing insights as to how they experience or view the game event.

Initially many observations were collected from a single basketball event. Observing a new basketball event at some point no longer produced very much new information, indicating that I had my basic material. Attending additional games allowed me to verify past observations and get maybe one or two new observations. After identifying areas that had been neglected, like recording what rabid fans yell, I found and collected a fair amount of additional observations.

The fan community connects Wyomingites, students, professors, and alumni. At one game I sat next to a fan from Cheyenne who has been attending UW basketball games since 1942 and actually saw the UW NCAA 1943 Championship team play in Half-Acre gym. Attending basketball games is a social event with attendant social scripts.

Another type of fan includes the pure sports fan or a rabid fan who is there only to experience the game, undaunted by the social potential of the event and who may yell offensive statements and/or obscenities quite loudly even when no one else is yelling. Amusing conversations by unknown fans nearby provide comic relief during boring games or while the action is paused.

As a fan of fans, the motivation behind my gaze (like the fan gaze but with one more level of looking) upon game events is surreptitious in nature despite being a spectator at a public spectacle. I reflected afterwards: Who are the characters on the stage of the basketball event? Where are they located culturally and spatially? These observations helped to illuminate exactly what is going on during fan attendance of UW Cowboy basketball games. Who do the various characters in the 'game event' represent? I believe fan behavior makes sense only within the 'game event' context. Another important aspect of the basketball event is place.[4] The event occurs in a certain physical location and has a particular role in the psyche of the fan.

The Arena Auditorium or AA, both the outside and the interior, including seats for fans and the basketball court itself, represents contested terrain. Two teams fight a battle to win the game while fans are restricted to off-court areas and must compete for closer seats. Fans obtain better seats and buy status through financial success or by choosing to donate money on joining the Cowboy Joe Club. Other approaches such as time management allows students to arrive early to take first-come first-served seats. To gain access to the basketball event a fan must be a character on the basketball event stage, be a student, or get a ticket. One problem that occurs is that students pay activity fees and can get into the game free while others must buy a seat. For a student and non-student to go to a game together the non-student must buy a ticket regardless. The student must either have the non-student sit in the student section or buy a seat next to the non-student. There are different qualifications to get in and seating policies that divide the arena into groups.

The first eight rows in the AA are special seats that cannot be had without donating five hundred dollars to the Cowboy Joe Club and buying season tickets, even if the season is almost already over. Rows nine through fourteen are also special seats requiring a fan to donate two hundred and fifty dollars to the Cowboy Joe Club. Even so, one cannot choose his or her seats. There is a lottery for that. Either some ticket buyers never go to games or there are some unsold seats left empty over multi-year periods. General ticket buyers are even told that for some games all the lower level seats are sold.

Noting that the application for buying season tickets does not mention the Cowboy Joe Club, I questioned this. The manager in the ticket booth informed me that the AA is not a public building and that the Cowboy Joe Club owns the building and that I *had to donate* to the Cowboy Joe Club. I did not like this answer either so I e-mailed the President of the University of Wyoming. The prompt reply I received, which was no doubt politically driven, was that this is the way it has always been. The ticket brochure now lists 'Cowboy Joe Donation.' Donation means voluntary, so technically one should be able to get good seats without donating. My quest to get access to good seating was stymied.

In fact, according to the Cowboy Joe Club office (766-6242) UW owns the Arena Auditorium while the Athletic Department operates it. Ticket policies are arrived at through joint discussions of the Athletic Department and the Cowboy Joe Club boards. For example, seats are gained based on priority points that represent past donations and seats purchased. Although rows one through twenty-five are completely sold out except for six single seats. The minimum donation to join the Cowboy Joe Club is fifty dollars.

The Cowboy Joe Club is a semi-official organization that seems to function like a private club with a private facility. Even so, the Cowboy Joe Club functions as a great tool to gather alumni into a special group. As UW basketball becomes more successful and commodified a democratizing pressure pushes the Cowboy Joe Club and the Athletic Department to be more inclusive in the attempt to diversify the fan base and increase revenue. The audience is self selected as some opt out (chose not to attend basketball events) to avoid loud and obnoxious fans, advertising, or supporting non-academic activities occurring on campus.

UW faculty and employees do get a discount on the price of season tickets. Game day tickets cost more than the season ticket amount. Many in rows one through fourteen do not buy things from concessions, but either bring food with them or eat before or after the game. So the total cost for two people to go to one game (or all home games) and sit in rows one through eight is five hundred dollars (Cowboy Joe club donation) plus three hundred and twelve (season tickets or two hundred and fifty dollars for faculty/staff) or eight hundred and twelve dollars. Face value for one conference game is fifteen dollars per seat.

The student section has rows one to fourteen for section K only (typically filled with 6th Man Club members, which mirrors the Cowboy Joe Club). The UW student band takes up section L front rows, and section J is where the players' ramp is. Even though row fifteen is next to row fourteen, there is a big difference in that row fourteen costs an extra two hundred and fifty dollars. Refer to Appendix 1 for a seating chart.

Apparently joining the Cowboy Joe Club through donation allows one the possibility of getting closer seats. The 1999-2000 application for Cowboy basketball tickets listed under the heading "Cowboy Joe Club Member," three boxes that could be checked. The boxes said 1) Yes, I support the program, 2) No, but would like information, 3) No interest. The 2000-2001 ticket brochure did not mention the Cowboy Joe Club. The 2001-2002 Cowboy Basketball ticket information lists Cowboy Joe Donation. The diagram of the AA in turn has sections color-coded with a note two hundred and fifty dollars or one hundred and twenty five-dollar donation per seat per year.

The UW athletics web site talks about the benefits of being a member of the Cowboy Joe Club. Membership entitles one to priority seating. One chart shows that a person can join for fifty dollars although all ticket information for basketball shows requirements of one hundred and twenty five or two hundred and fifty per seat.

By donating a calf for an auction, one can get most of the benefits too. Member ranches get their name and ranch listed on plaques displayed throughout the AA concourse. For a donation of ten thousand dollars, one can get invited to special events, travel with the football team, and get an on-field presentation.[5]

Wyoming is not the only collegiate institution that provides special access to those with money. Though maybe it is the only one that accepts steers. In his book on college basketball John Feinstein talks about larger issues in college basketball revolving around Duke. In one section he talks about some of the evolution of the sport of basketball and the changing of who gets access to what seats as follows:

> More and more, as big money has come into college basketball, arenas have been built with plush, expensive seats close to the court. The big-money contributors sit in these seats; the only thing that can get them on their feet is the national anthem and, perhaps, the need to go to the bathroom at halftime. This is not the case at Duke. Downstairs is for the students; the bleachers are within a few feet of the court. Given this proximity, the students believe it is their *obligation* to play a role in the outcome of the game. Their participation goes well beyond noise. If an opponent

has had the misfortune to get into some kind of trouble before playing at Duke, heaven help him. (Feinstein, 1990, p. 20)

Even so the Cowboy Joe Club members and the 6th Man Club members are important to the basketball event, as these are the fans with the money, social status, and the dedication to travel to see away games and provide needed financial, psychic, auditory, and physical support for the team.

Perhaps the closer, more expensive, seats do not have the best view. Some professional football stadium managers have discovered that seats on the second level provide better views (and so charge three times or more for seats higher up and further away from the field) just as seats on the twenty-five yard line provide more and closer action than does the fifty yard line. In the AA, seats in or near row twenty-five are next to the portals and so allow quick entrance and exit as well as closer access to concessions and bathrooms. An argument could also be made that the view of the basketball event is superior in row twenty-five as opposed to sitting closer in the Cowboy Joe Club areas—rows one through fourteen.

UW Basketball History

Wyoming basketball has a long history full of traditions for the basketball event. In 1943, they won the National Collegiate Athletic Association (NCAA) and National Invitation Tournaments (NIT), played in the NIT championship game in 1986, and made it to the sweet sixteen in 1987.

I should define terms. The current game of college basketball was formed partially by a University of Wyoming basketball event. The game of basketball refers to the rules, technicalities, and actual playing of the game. A basketball event includes the game and everything immediately surrounding it while the sport of basketball includes all basketball events.

Wyoming has its role in basketball history: one good one (jump shot); one bad one (racism). Kenny Sailors of Hillsdale, Wyoming, invented the jump shot while playing for the University of Wyoming during the early 1940's. Prior to this, players shot while standing flat-footed rather than jumping.

Another piece of UW's history, dealing with racism, is relevant to the basketball event even though it is centered on football. This is important to help explain the UW fan behavior of taunting BYU. At the time of this event UW had many African Americans on their football team while BYU had none. UW had a very good football team and the team's African American players wanted to protest against BYU's and the Mormon Church's racist policies.[6]

A legacy of racial tensions that came to light in the Black 14 incident during the 1960s featuring the football team, a protest against BYU, and a reaction on the part of UW administration may explain why there's yelling at BYU during UW basketball games. This could also affect the relationship of mostly white fans to a team on which African Americans are significantly represented. (Larson, 1978, p. 593).[7] This historical event may help to explain why UW students taunt BYU with vulgar chants during the basketball event.[8]

The only official roles played by women at the basketball event are those of UW cheerleader (virtually all of the cheerleaders are white), a member of the wildfire dance troupe, singer of the National Anthem, a UW band member, a technical assistant to a male television announcer, or organizer of fan contests. Women can join the 6th Man club. Minorities are predominately relegated to staff or blue-collar work. Virtually all Cowboy Joe Club fans are white, despite the local community's having a minority population.[9]

My Basketball Experience

In the oil camp where I grew up, with a population of only a few dozen, there were indoor and outdoor basketball courts, along with boys and girls teams. (Pitcher, 2001, pp. 68,94) One of my earliest memories is of four kids there: two were six-foot five and two were six-foot eight. They played basketball. This helped to make me want to play basketball. The basketball event for some fans, like myself, may begin the first time a basketball is held in one's hands.

My experience with being a character on the basketball event stage begins in high school, where I was a player, team manager, team-captain, and a referee. One summer while attending the basketball camp sponsored by UW, I met several coaches. Playing basketball was fun, but I rarely watched games on TV or went to games. I never looked up to athletes, or saw them as heroes.

As a fan of UW men's basketball I have collected some memorabilia and memories. While attending the 50-year team reunion banquet held at UW in 1993, I met Kenny Sailors, the inventor of the jump shot. I was at the first game ever played in the AA on February 20, 1982, which had a sell out crowd, and saw on TV and recorded their 1987 NCAA victory putting them in the sweet sixteen. That game is one of the finest moments in UW basketball event history other than the 1943 NCAA Championship win and this year's win over the 6th ranked Gonzaga, in the first round of the NCAA tournament. This win was as exciting as watching the Denver Bronco's finally win their first Super Bowl. I have a basketball autographed by former UW players, many of whom were drafted into the NBA: Charles Bradley, Anthony Johnson, Bill Garnett, Mike Jackson, Kenneth Ollie, Chris Engler, and the rest of the team members they played with.

Through a brief participation in college basketball I experienced some of the pressures faced by athletes. My freshman year at the University of Wyoming, I took beginning basketball for physical education. The basketball teacher just happened to be the UW Junior Varsity head coach and he announced tryouts for the team. He said I should give it a go. I did and I made the team as the number three guard behind the two returning starters. We usually practiced at Corbett Gym, but we did practice sometimes in the Arena Auditorium (AA). The wood floor in the AA has good spring to it and is easy on the knees compared to non-wood courts. The showers, designed for collegiate players, had the knobs for turning the water on so high up I could barely reach them.

At first practices were in the evening, but the team voted to start having practice in the afternoon. This meant that I would have to skip classes in order to attend practice. I would have to choose between my education and playing on the team. And so I quit the team. I did keep stats for a couple JV games after that though.

I understand the vocabulary or 'rules of the game,' although superficially, in coaching terms through taking courses on the theory of coaching basketball as research for this Thesis. Some of the current UW assistant coaches, graduate assistants, trainers, etc, participated in the basketball class, providing insight from other angles into the basketball event.

Structure of this Thesis

This Chapter talked about my new role as ethnographer and analyst, imagined communities, defining the term basketball event, the power of place, UW basketball history, and the author's background. My second chapter will look at what occurs during a particular University of Wyoming basketball game, or basketball event, organized or framed as a structured narrative with a distinct sequence and hierarchy, both scripted and collective, made up of key moments, imagined communities, and various voices emerging from and reflecting off fans. I take the point of view that fans are in fact cheering for themselves; this helps to explain fan behavior. My feelings, reactions, and emotional responses to moments like the national anthem, or a steal and a slam will be discussed along with a personal analysis. I will discuss commercials, the 6th man club, the Cotton-Eyed Joe phenomenon, and where fans are located.

My third chapter extends my observations of the basketball event in a participant observation mini-ethnography over several basketball game events. This is where I attempt to switch from being a participant to an observer. The point of view taken is more from that of a detached observer looking for patterns to emerge. New or unusual moments as well as observations that are consistent over a number of basketball events will be explored.

Notes for Chapter One

[1] Another influence shaping the methodology for this study is Thorstein Veblin's 1899, *Theory of the Leisure Class*. This idea although over one hundred years old is a timeless concept that applies not just to Fandom in particular but to many texts in general.

> [T]he data employed to illustrate or enforce the argument have by preference been drawn from everyday life, by direct observation or through common notoriety, rather than from more recondite sources at a farther remove. It is hoped that no one will find his sense of literary or scientific fitness offended by this recourse to homely facts, or by what may at times appear to be a callous freedom in handling vulgar phenomena…Such premises and corroborative evidence as are drawn from remoter sources, as well as whatever articles of theory or inference are borrowed from ethnological science, are also of the more familiar and accessible kind and should be readily traceable to their source by fairly well-read persons. The usage of citing sources and authorities has therefore not been observed. Likewise the few quotations that have been introduced, chiefly by way of illustration, are also such as will commonly be recognized with sufficient facility without the guidance of citation. (Veblen, 1998, p. x)

[2] In his influential essay "Thick Description: Toward an Interpretive Theory of Culture (1973)," Clifford Geertz explains why so many pages must be filled to try and explain a simple observation (like that of seeing a fan 'cheering for self' at a 'basketball event.') When one sees someone wink, was their eye merely twitching or were they winking at someone?

> …a fair sense of how much goes into ethnographic description of even the most elemental sort—how extraordinarily "thick" it is. In finished anthropological writings, including those collected here, this fact—that what we call our data are really our own constructions of other people's constructions of what they and their compatriots are up to—is obscured because most of what we need to comprehend a particular event, ritual, custom, idea, or whatever is insinuated as background information before the thing itself is directly examined…there is nothing particularly wrong with this, and it is in any case inevitable. But it does lead to a view of anthropological research as rather more of an observational and rather less of an interpretive activity than it really is. Right down at the factual base, the hard rock, insofar as there is any, of the whole enterprise, we are already explicating: and worse, explicating explications. Winks upon winks upon winks. (Geertz, 1973, p. 9)

[3] The quotation that follows uses 'nation' as an example of a larger realm of meaning.

> Finally, it is imagined as a *community*, because, regardless of the actual inequality and exploitation that may prevail in each, the nation is

always conceived as a deep, horizontal comradeship. Ultimately it is this fraternity that makes it possible, over the past two centuries, for so many millions of people, not so much to kill, as willingly to die for such limited imaginings. (Anderson, 1983, p. 7)

[4] Dolores Hayden in her book *The Power of Place: Urban Landscapes as Public History* although not about sports describes the connection between culture and place:

"The power of place—the power of ordinary urban landscapes to nurture citizens' public memory, to encompass shared time in the form of shared territory..." (Hayden, 1995, p. 9)

[5] The UW athletics web site explains what the Cowboy Joe Club is: (http://wyomingathletics.fansonly.com/boosters/boosters-static-info/booster-overview.html). [www.uwyo.edu]

The Cowboy Joe Club was formed in 1970 as the main fund raising arm of the University of Wyoming's Intercollegiate Athletic program. The Club is a non-profit organization with a member base of almost 3,300 fans from throughout the United States and all over the world. With your assistance, the Cowboy Joe Club can help fund scholarships, academic counseling, summer school, books, and other needed projects. Thanks to you, these exceptional student-athletes will have the opportunity to fulfill their dreams in brown and gold. (UW, 2002)

[6] Coach Eaton had the power to enforce his discipline on the "Black Fourteen." Wyoming was brought face to face with its self-image as the Equality State when the Black Fourteen stood up for their rights and refused to accept the dominant culture's rule and refused to assimilate.

When the black fourteen players showed up in the coach's office sporting black armbands, Coach Eaton told them that their football scholarships were cancelled and that they were done playing for Wyoming because they had violated the coaching rule, and for wanting to wear black armbands at the coming Wyoming vs. BYU game

[7] To see a video clip (two minutes and eighteen seconds) of those protesting the Black Fourteen incident go to:
http://uwadmnweb.uwyo.edu/ahc/digital/qtfiles/BLACK14.MOV. (AHC, 2002)

[8] Refer to Chapter Two for descriptions of what students chant and some of the things that rabid fans yell out during the 'basketball event.'

[9] "Most of the fans who get in to see Indiana and Kentucky play are white. Most of the players they watch are black. When a truly gifted white player comes along, he quickly becomes a hero to the white fans." (Feinstein, 1988, pp 104-5).

Chapter Two:

A Narrative Script of the Basketball Event

> The location of his gaze falls within the general domain of covert surveillance, and the object of his observation is the fully exposed act of naïve, deluded looking. At least in a metaphorical sense, he sees their eyes but they do not see his. Their mistake about his location...is the folk narrative's literalization of the deeper fact that the naïve gaze not only mistakes the object of its desire, it also misperceives the gaze of an Other, taking it for neutral, benign, and, most of all, directed at something remote rather than at their own act of faulty looking. (Dorst, 1999, p. 15)

The Conclusion Briefly Stated

Fans cheer for self indirectly. Fans cheer for the team that they identify with. Through the process of 'cheering for self' while attending the basketball event people are taught how to become fans, to consume a UW product the basketball event—and to consume advertisers' products.

Geography of the Arena

Inside the basketball arena, called the Arena Auditorium or AA, there is a division of space through imaginary borders.[1] Some areas are for characters on the stage of the basketball event—players, coaches, referees, and cheerleaders. Other areas are for students only or Cowboy Joe Club members only. One area is for kids eighteen and under, another for fans of the other team, the rest for others that do not fit in any other category.

The Rochelle athletics center, located next to the AA, is named for Curtis and Marian Rochelle who donated over four million dollars towards the building's cost. As at many public universities, one of UW's largest private donations has gone for athletics and not for academic buildings, professors, or academic student scholarships. Varsity scholarships for athletes provide room, board, tuition, books and tutors. In contrast, Wyoming High School Honor scholarships for top academic students provide for in-state tuition only. For an out-of-state athlete, this is worth over five times what in-state scholars get from UW.

Parking spaces normally for students near the AA, Fine Arts Center, and College of Law are reserved during games, probably for the press and Cowboy Joe Club members during games. The parking lot to the east of the AA has signs saying "Permit Parking Only." By the AA, during some basketball events, there is a HumVee (modern army jeep) parked with "Outback Steakhouse" painted on it.

The Arena Auditorium provides fans with a position located above the basketball court so that their gaze is from a superior position looking down upon the game. The landscape is similar for all fans, as the AA is round. The AA is like a giant living room, making it possible to pick out people in sections all around the building. The court is rectangular so that seats perpendicular to half-court provide a better view than seats behind one basket and far from the other basket. This arena was designed to provide vantage points, although unequal, for fans to gaze upon the game and from which to experience the basketball event.

Some seats provide views where some action is blocked by the backboard, or are so far from the court as to be annoying for the near-sighted or for those who lack the height to see over the UW band members and their instruments. The press is located at court level, even with the action. On-court special guests may even look up to the action. Students sit at mid-court, as do Cowboy Joe Club members, but on opposite sides from each other.[2]

Perhaps having an elevated position physically helps to facilitate fans' urge to yell at those on the court and for rabid fans to feel empowered to yell foul things to all who get in their way. Audio from the loudspeakers emanate from above, while the U.S. Flag is located superior to all persons in the arena. Commercials displayed on the Jumbotron (large video display for fans) also come from a position above that of all fans.[3]

During the basketball event one can see a snapshot of the process of cultural categorization, reflecting unequal distribution of power along the dimensions of age, class, race, and gender. If one knows a fans' age, race, class, and gender, one can almost tell where the fan will be sitting and his or her potential roles. In effect age, race, class, and gender segregate people. Bobby Knight once told a wanna-be assistant coach (woman) who asked what she should do he told her to change her gender. And even though this was flippant and glib, there is a lot of truth to it.

Women's teams are no different though in that those with women head coaches often end up with all women assistants.

Where a particular fan sits reveals that fans' class status, if not power. Students sit in their section. Upper class people sit in the first fourteen rows. Middle class people sit in the rows behind row fourteen. Lower class and others sit in the upper level. Kids sit in the knothole section. Lower class people man the concessions and do the labor.

Closer seats held by those in the Cowboy Joe Club can mean people might sit next to each other for decades. Sitting in the student section, though, has its own advantages. By arriving at different times and choosing different seats, the student fan can view the basketball event from different angles and sit near a different mix of fans for each game, other than those fans that actually came together as a group.

The 6th Man Club is made up of UW students who pay twelve dollars to get a 6th Man Club t-shirt and the right to enter games thirty minutes before anyone else, get closer seats, eat some complementary pizza, receive a free rally towel, and have sent to them an electronic newsletter. Students who come to the game in their t-shirt are similar to referees and players wearing their uniform to the game. The 6th Man Club t-shirt in effect is a uniform for serious student fans. Student fans go to watch student athletes.

The 6th Man Club parallels the Cowboy Joe Club. Many 6th Man Club students stand during the entire game, forcing all those sitting higher up in the arena to stand also, in order to see the game. One section, to the left of the die-hard 6th Man Club members and behind the band, is filled with students that refuse to stand the entire game.

Being a corporation, or at least representing one, or being part of an imagined community affords special access. Advertising and sponsoring the basketball event provide special access for the products of manufacturers and those who run the corporations.

There are fourteen people at the press and scorer's table on the floor, including the UW Director of Sports Information and the local radio station sports announcer, both covering the game. The local paper's sports writer sits there too. The press table is at mid-court between the two team benches. Two more rows of press take up a specially designed area that would have been the first four rows of seats for fans. The first row has twenty-five people with twenty-one more behind them. PC monitors abound, as do notebook computers. A couple of laser printers sit at one end. One woman seems to be delivering faxes and messages every once in a while. Fans who identify with the basketball event have their 'cheering for self' facilitated through press members. As the press seems to be there to record and describe the basketball event for a particular individual fan, the point of view is one as if the fan was the teams owner. Fans are told what they want to hear i.e. that they matter and it is their own personal team.

The steps used to walk from entrance portals to either upper or lower seating provide a borderland between the various sections, for example, separating students and Cowboy Joe Club members. An imaginary line is drawn between fans and the characters on the stage of the basketball event. Another imaginary line separates Cowboy Joe Club members from non-members, who sit behind rows one through fourteen.

Between the segregated seating areas, and also in the segregated parking areas, are common areas. A walking path just inside of the arena makes a complete circle around the arena and is lined with bathrooms and concessions. There are separate entrances for the characters on the stage of the basketball event.

Hanging up high at one end of the AA are flags or banners representing good years, such as when UW was Conference champion. One banner is for when UW's men's basketball team won, in overtime, the NCAA National Championship in 1943.[4] (AHC, 2002) On top of the backboard, which holds the basketball hoop, is the shot clock and game time device. This device has three rectangular faces directed in different directions for fans in different sections to see. Combined, the three faces make up a triangle. Two shot clocks display the time left before a shot must be taken or the time left in the current period. There is also a big red light to signal that the period is over. The shot clock on backboards is in red, while the time left in the game on backboards is in green. The text for the shot clock time is larger than the text for the game time.

The regular scoreboards show time left in the game and period (one or two) indicators in yellow. The total number of team fouls, the possession arrow, and the score are displayed in red. The player number and the number of fouls for that particular player are displayed in green. The score and team fouls have the same text size.

One clock, showing Mountain Standard Time, is up high in the AA opposite the Jumbotron. There is a big flag above the knothole section that says, "Knot Hole." Two old unused scoreboards opposite each other are near the top of the AA from mid court with the name of a sponsor from the past: Conoco. There are so many ads that competitors do not have exclusivity. Two different cellular phone companies have ads.

Regardless of the number of fans the entertainment is similar other than perhaps the relative noise level. There is in fact little difference between there being a few more fans or a few less fans or even between only one fan or sixteen thousand fans.[5] One fan can view the entire basketball event from one physical point. Although game stats, ads, the game itself etc are there for all to see, a fan never feels that someone else is seeing or experiencing something that he or she is not.

The fans have everything directed at them as individuals. Virtually everything supports the fans assumption that he or she matters. A fans identification with the team and basketball event is supported and fans' 'cheering for self' come naturally. Each fan hears and sees essentially the same things. Rarely does a fan have to ask someone else what happened or for information. Fans do not ask others about their team. It is my team or our team. The personal and unique identification of each fan with the event provides the basis for the fan to cheer for self by yelling, booing and consuming.

Ads may be heard over the loudspeakers, seen on the Jumbotron, or displayed throughout the arena. Some ads move around or are manually manipulated. Other ads are experienced through participation. Purchased programs contain even more ads. Ads are everywhere to be seen, heard, and experienced. Corporate and institutional logos, trademarks, and names abound. The walking slice of Papa John's Pizza seems to be the de-facto mascot of the University of Wyoming Cowboys since there is no other person dressed up as something and walking around.

Tip off is controlled by clock time outside the AA environment. But once the whistle blows, sense of time is surrendered to game time, which is indicated on the game clock. The one thing during the basketball event that occurs at a certain time is the tip off, which begins the game. No one knows for sure when halftime will be or when the game will end, but the tip off is delayed only if the other team cannot make it over the summit because the roads are closed due to bad weather. Fans will know at the end of the game who won and by how much.

All fans want to see the game and are united through the U.S. flag and standing for the anthem, physically at least. Fans identify with what they want, for example, a particular team to win (despite the fact that some fans are for the other team), the school the team represents, a product (Pepsi). Fans may tune out and/or ignore what they do not like and assume other fans identify with the same products, film clips, or songs. A fan enjoying and cheering for products like Pepsi or UW that he or she likes is in effect 'cheering for self.'

Within the AA, there are Hall of Fame displays showing great teams, great players, and great coaches from the past. I look up Kenny Sailers and the 1943 Championship team. Kenny used to practice his shot in an empty parking lot next to the apartment where I live. One of the Championship team members made his career as a teacher at the local high school. Former Head Coach Jim Brandenburg as well as superstar player Fennis Dembo have plaques, too.

'The Basketball Event'[6]

The basketball event provides suspense in that the eventual winner is not known in advance, but otherwise most event elements are familiar and predictable. A typical game lasts two hours from tip off to finish. The basketball event, from the time a local fan leaves home until he returns is about four hours.

Pre-Game

Driving to the AA, or the "Dome of Doom," at the University of Wyoming, I listen to the pregame show on the radio to get some hints on what to expect at the game and some audio from the coach. Some people have parking spaces marked with their names east of the AA and north of the new Rochelle Athletic Center, a facility built in large part with private donations. I park in front of married student housing and walk to the AA, thus avoiding paying ten-dollars to park at the AHC or five dollars to park in mud and snow in an unlit parking area.

After having my UW ID scanned and before I proceed to find a seat in the open seating student section, I pass a table with UW clothes—hats and shirts with the new colors (prairie gold and brown) and trinkets—then I head to a concession stand. Paying the exorbitant prices, I buy a hot dog, soda, and a game program (eleven dollars). Fans identify with UW and so buy and wear things to identify their self as "UW." After a fans team wins, sales go up on logos of the team to wear or display. This phenomenon helps to demonstrate fans 'cheering for self.'

After finding a seat, the fan has nowhere to put a coat other than on the chair. The seats, especially once all are full, force the fan to sit rigidly facing the basketball court by making looking in other directions uncomfortable. After consuming my hot dog, I place my drink under my chair. The loudspeakers that hang near the catwalk and inside the ring of lights at the top of the center of the dome inform fans that Outback Steakhouse is the sponsor of this game. Fans who enjoy the basketball event and steaks now may link the two. Vegetarians or those who do not eat red meat may not make a positive connection but are given many other opportunities to find identification with other products along with their team and a reason to cheer for self.

From the first moment the visiting team members come into the arena they are made fun of, booed, and yelled at. As the other team comes in the UW band plays the "Looney Tunes" theme. An informant watching the game pointed this out to me.

Players, cheerleaders, and Wildfire members do warm-up stretches out on the floor. Next the players do warm-ups and drills before simply shooting around. One fan informant that attended a game with me noted that she felt the cheerleaders should be able to wear pants and a shirt of their choosing instead of a short skirt. Another non-fan noted that cheerleading has become a sport in itself, requiring these performers to be athletes. One can easily assume that the cheerleaders enjoy their role and not consider that they might like to have other options or roles to play in the basketball event. Having no personal identification with being a cheerleader this escaped me until it was pointed out. Cheerleaders provide an opportunity for women fans to identify with some characters on the basketball event stage and to then cheer for self.

The press is assembled in their area near the floor with attendant notebook computers, faxes, and printers. One row of seats along a table on the floor is filled with twenty special guests who seem to be regular folks, perhaps friends or family of the athletic department. Team chairs to the right of the scorer's table have ads for Outback Steak House on them. All of the scorers are white men. Behind the chairs are Gatorade coolers. The coach has a small Gatorade cup that he sips out of once in a while, leaving it on the scorers' bench. This act makes Gatorade very visible in the arena and also on screen in televised games.

After their initial drills, the University of Wyoming players leave the arena for a little while. The University of Wyoming band plays a song in between the songs being broadcast over the loudspeakers. The band members wear brown and yellow shirts with horizontal stripes over their clothes. City of Laramie and UW policemen stand in each of two tunnels leading into the sports arena. On the four corners of the court, as well as in the two tunnels, stand security personnel wearing red jackets. The four security people on the court stand facing the crowd scanning for trouble and troublemakers.

A cheerleader runs into the AA and around the basketball court with a large banner made up of UW colors with a cowboy and bucking horse on it. The UW players run into the arena immediately behind the banner. As the players come back, the UW fight song, "Ragtime Cowboy Joe" is played and most fans stand up and clap to the beat. Fans who identify with UW or the UW team yell to demonstrate the connection and in effect cheer for self. The UW fight song is played before the game starts, at the end of the first half, before the second half and after the game is over. Sometimes when the basketball event is going really well, or very poorly, this song is played more often. Listening to this same song over and over can get tiring. Few seem to know the words but some fans do actually know and sing the song.[7]

Over the loudspeaker fans are admonished to use no foul language, throw no objects onto the floor, behave, exhibit good sportsmanship and fair play, and show respect or risk being ejected. Fans are also admonished to be prepared to exit the AA in a safe and timely manner should the need arise, no doubt due to the tragedy of September 11, 2001. The overhead loudspeakers for the basketball event talk with faceless authority like from a supreme being to the individual fan. Commercials coming from this same point source may subconsciously seem authoritative. This helps to make each fan the same but also a dominated individual in a passive role. Later fans will cheer for self.

A rap song is played over the loudspeakers. There is also an announcement that so and so needs to report to the first aid station. Parts of various types of songs (e.g. 'Cotton-Eyed Joe,' 'YMCA,' 'Who Let the Dogs Out,' and 'Twist and Shout,') that should individually appeal to all the various generations are played over the course of the basketball event. Two people sweep the basketball floor. Assistant coaches now sit on the University of Wyoming bench. Referees mill about, wearing black shoes and solid black pants along with vertically striped black and white shirts, waiting for the game to start. The University of Wyoming basketball team huddles together on court and begins to jump in unison.

This basketball event is going to be on live TV so two male announcers talk into a camera while standing on the court before game starts. The TV announcers then sit at the special guest table near courtside, but opposite the scorers' table. Even though they are sitting right there and can see the basketball event live with their own eyes they have two ten inch TV screens, presumably so they know what TV viewers are seeing. Two women sit on the outside of the two male announcers, apparently in technical roles.

One UW policeman and one Laramie policeman walk down the steps and then over into the crowd to a particular fan who just sat down. They escort him out of the arena.

The University of Wyoming Reserve Officer Training Corps (UW ROTC) presents the colors: the U.S. Flag, the Wyoming State Flag, and the Air Force flag. Everyone is told to stand and show respect for his or her country and flag. Everyone in the building stands and listens as a woman sings the National Anthem. This rendition must be live; the anthem played over the loudspeakers from a recording just does not evoke the same emotions. A large U.S. flag and a large Wyoming State flag hang from the top of the Arena Auditorium (AA) in the center of the artificial lights and near a group of loudspeakers. A simulated waving flag shows on the Jumbotron. The simulated flag seems so phony. Many fans express dissatisfaction with the video flag. Even so this moment of singing the National Anthem for me is the most stirring part. Just before the end of the anthem, a group of four new ads are flipped by a device so as to be visible by the Cowboy Joe Club crowd that is opposite the student section. These ads consist of corporate logos and appear to be about one foot high and two feet wide. As the song ends, cheerleaders are flipped in the air.

Players for the opposing team are announced. The other team's players get booed as they are introduced. Fans yell out "Hi" along with the player's number or name. One player gets heckled by fans because the announcer refers to him as "Dilrod." In fact the player's name was really "Dalron" not "Dilrod." Another player with a unique hairdo is asked, "Who cut your hair?" Every player and coach on the opposing team is white.

The UW starting players, head coach, and assistant coaches are announced. Wyoming's players are cheered as they are introduced. Counting the players on injured reserve and two ineligible transfer players, UW has approximately half minority players. The team has one head coach and three assistant coaches, one of which is of a minority. One University of Wyoming starter seems to elicit boos along with cheers. The "boos" are really "ooooh's." The players have their number and the word "Wyoming" on the front of their jersey and their last name and number on the back. Cheerleaders and/or Wildfire members chant over and over: 'Let's go Cowboys' in perfect unison and monotone. A walking slice of Papa John's pizza moves about on the edge of the floor. Every few minutes, the ads in front of the special guests' table are flipped to show other ads. A special song with no lyrics is played loudly signaling to everyone that the game is about to begin.

Approximately twenty-one people are on the UW bench. These include the head coach, assistants, graduate assistants, red-shirt players, transfer players—who by NCAA regulations must sit out one year—and the regular players. A team is allowed to have fifteen scholarship players. There is almost a one-to-one ratio between players and staff. Corporate ads intrude into the actual play of the game through the "Media timeouts" so that TV and radio coverage can get in lots of extra advertising. Sponsors are announced and fans are encouraged to do business with them.

Once the game starts, everyone's focus and gaze is upon the basketball. Fans, referees, players, coaches, and all others know the action that matters is centered on the basketball. Advertisers other than UW and its team within the basketball event try to capture and hold onto everyone's eyes whenever the game is paused.

First-Half

While "Are You Ready to Rumble" is blasted over the loudspeakers, the game begins with a jump ball.[8] Everywhere I look there are ads, logos, trademarks, and names for corporations and UW. The basketball floor itself has painted advertising for UW, Pepsi, and the Mountain West Conference (MWC). The Jumbotron displays ads and the loudspeaker inundates one's ears with ads. One loudspeaker ad wants fans to spend twenty dollars in Cheyenne at a liquor store in order to get a free six-pack of water. An informant wonders if there have been any takers.

Someone dressed up as a slice of Papa John's Pizza wanders the court. The Papa John's Pizza Scream, a very loud moment, is when fans yell and then some are handed a pizza box by a UW Cheerleader running up into the crowd. Often a specific person known by the Cheerleader gets the pizza in the crowd, as evidenced by the Cheerleader coming up into the crowd earlier during the basketball event to make sure the person sticks around and to have a brief chat indicating familiarity. After UW makes a three-point basket, a free t-shirt is thrown or shot by a special gun into the crowd.

The only time the loyal 6th Man Club sits is during timeouts. The 6th man t-shirt has four corporate logos on the back (AND 1—sells basketball shoes and uniforms, Brown and Gold—sells UW logo clothing, Pepsi—which has a contract for exclusive marketing at UW, and Mix 105.5—plays music for a younger audience). Student fans become ads for corporate logos revealing a non-fan reason for the 6th Man Club. The logos are highly visible to those sitting or standing behind 6th Man Club members—*when the 6th Man Club members wearing the 6th Man Club t-shirt are standing*. Incidentally the 6th Man Club was started by part of the Athletic Department's basketball staff. Other similar clubs exist so perhaps the phenomenon is encouraged by corporations. I wear mine over the top of another shirt. The core group of 6th Man Club members is hard-core, rabid, almost fanatical fans. During halftime, the UW Athletic Director (AD) gives some 6th Man Club members copies of halftime stats. I manage to get a copy to take home. The 6th Man Club winner of a trip to Las Vegas for the MWC tournament is announced. I hope I do not win, wanting to avoid attracting too much attention to myself.[9]

During some timeouts the Cheerleaders try to get those in the student section to yell 'Cowboys' followed by trying to get fans sitting on the opposite side of the arena to yell the same. The informal contest is to see which group yells the loudest.

The coach calls a timeout, so the 6th Man Club members sit down. Replays are shown on the Jumbotron. A clip from the film Patton plays on the Jumbotron: "We're going to go through you like crap through a goose." The playing of film clips help to keep the audience's gaze fused on a common point during pauses in game action. Six coaches huddle on the floor away from the players, presumably so assistant coaches can tell the coach what they think without the players hearing. If the head coach agrees he will tell the players momentarily and the message will come with some likelihood that it was the coach's idea. The coach substitutes a lot, so many players get substantial playing time.

During some timeouts the cheerleaders, or Wildfire, perform on the floor to music. Wildfire members, while performing to music, leap into the air, landing on the floor in the splits position and drawing an awed reaction from the crowd. An injured player for the other team gets cheered when he gets up and walks off the floor. Another timeout results in a fan contest on the floor. Bowling with frozen turkeys as part of one fan contest on the hard wood court makes one cringe for the floor's sake. Some big-time fans wear radio headsets to get the radio play by play and commentary. Local and national TV crews cover the game. Two TV cameras are on the floor and there are at least two in the stands.

Halftime

The first half of the game is over and Wildfire storms the floor, performing to a warm reception. Wildfire is a dance group of women who dress and dance more provocatively than cheerleaders. Wildfire performs in a professional manner, with perfect synchronization.[10] Also during halftime in this game, a UW cheerleader runs up into the audience and sits on the lap of a nearby fan, apparently her boyfriend, for about ten minutes. She eats a hotdog. The boyfriend, who sits directly in front of us, wears a beat-up cowboy hat and has been waving it during the first half for some unknown reason. Now it appears it was to get her attention. A buddy of his had previously purchased two hotdogs and two sodas for him. Soon after her visit she is back on the floor doing flips.

Another fan contest entertains the crowd. Following that, athletes in street clothes go out onto the floor to be recognized for getting Cowboy Joe Club scholarships. Small kids, about four years old, run to half court and each puts on an oversized basketball shirt and shorts and a football helmet. The kids get into a toy car and race to the end of the court in an attempt to win. Kiss cam (a camera providing live video for the Jumbotron) scans the crowd. When two people are shown on the Jumbotron they are supposed to notice and then kiss each other. The floor is swept again. Corporate logos for AND 1 are even on the basketball hoop supports.

Two small kids sit at the foot of the hoop supports with towels ready to wipe the floors as necessary during game stoppages. One cameraman has a chair to the side of the end court. Photographers wander the end court taking still-photos. Wildfire stands at one end of the court cheering and moving, but motionless during actual game play except to yell for the team. The loudspeaker music, or whatever is playing, is turned off any time the game resumes.

Hall of fame players and coaches from the past are introduced on the floor. About fifty lettermen are invited to celebrate the 20th anniversary of the AA.

Former U.S. Senator for Wyoming, Alan Simpson, UW professor Dr. Pete Simpson (former player who is now a Professor), American Studies alumnus Mike Amundson, Anthony Johnson (now a UW policeman), Charles Bradley who played in early 80's and coached as an assistant in 86-87, and former Head Coach Jim Brandenburg who coached during the eighties, are present.

The other team is booed as they arrive to warm up for the second half. Some individuals from the opposing team are personally singled out for verbal abuse by rabid fans. Songs, ads, and some game statistics are heard over the loudspeaker. The UW fight song is played and most stand and clap. The Director of Intercollegiate Athletics for UW (AD or Athletic Director) gives some 6th Man Club members in the front row copies of halftime statistics.

There is absolutely no break—when the game is not underway there are ads, Jumbotron events, or on-the-floor activities. This is new to basketball in the last twenty years, a product of the sort of fragmented, mediated world that we live in. No dead air, no chance to think or reflect. Fans have little time to converse with other fans. Surrounding the basketball game within the basketball event are pseudo-events such as fan contests during halftime.

Second Half

The second half of the basketball game begins. During a timeout, "YMCA", "Twist and Shout", and "Who Let the Dogs Out" are heard. A slam-dunk, blocked shot, three-point basket and a rebound cause the fans to yell successively louder. Watching a team that you identify with play basketball allows one to vicariously relive previous experiences of actually playing the game. Perhaps fans who never actually played official games but that identify with the team also get to feel the same feelings as those actually playing the game. The emotion evoked by actually scoring points yourself, as a player in a game, in my experience, is very similar to the emotion felt when watching your team (i.e. a player you identify with) score. Then a foul ruins the pandemonium as silence spreads over the crowd.

Snippets of films and TV series are shown on the Jumbotron. The Cheers episode where one cast member taps a pencil until the other cast members join in is played on the Jumbotron. In response, Cowboy fans are expected to clap in unison and at an increasing rate. Another movie clip shows an injured Cowboy in a hospital bed, probably a bull rider, being told to "Cowboy Up." Whenever the game is close this clip is played. One referee sits on the scorer's table while three are on the court. The coach signals the crowd to get louder and they do. Some fans hold up a homemade sign saying: "God is a Cowboy." Fans who identify with Cowboys cheer i.e. 'cheering for self.'

One of the other team's players and one of UW's players get into a skirmish, pushing and shoving each other after a foul and timeout are called. The UW player gets a technical foul called on him; he is ejected from the game and must leave the arena. Furious fans, who take the penalty personally, boo at the referees. The other team gets to shoot two free throws and then gets to take the ball out. While the player shoots no one can stand on the same half of the court as him. Fans scream and yell while he misses the first one. The second free throw goes in, silencing the crowd.

With around seven minutes left in the game, one rather robust UW band member holds up his hand to one of his ears and then the other trying to get the fans to yell loud to the song "Cotton-Eyed Joe." When they are loud enough he begins to dance to the song. When he tires he stops again and tries to get the crowd loud again. Kids are seen imitating him rather than the players. Men and even a woman in a halter-top dance like him, too, while briefly appearing on the Jumbotron. Cotton-Eyed Joe, wearing bib-overalls, first thrusts his left leg up and to the left and then his right leg up and to the right. He continuously repeats these actions.

The new hero, and now legend, that started this emerging tradition, or at least is continuing or recreating previous similar antics of other band members during earlier seasons, is shown on the Jumbotron and has been featured in the local newspaper. Most fans stand up and clap while Cotton-Eyed Joe dances. While attending one UW basketball event at the Casper Events Center with a buddy, one fan stated that the main reason she goes to games is to see "Cotton-Eyed Joe," the UW band member who steps out of his role of band member to dance to the song "Cotton-Eyed Joe." Some student fans begin to quietly chant "bull-shit" along with the song.

During another timeout the loudspeaker tells fans to check to see if their game program is signed. If so, the fan has won two meals at a chain restaurant. A sticker under one's seat can win the fan something too. During this timeout fans also shoot baskets on the floor to see who can make the most points in thirty seconds and thus win prizes from Pepsi. The fans are even required to wear a Pepsi t-shirt while on the floor, but the shirt has to be returned after the contest. Part of the movie "Tommy Boy" is featured on the Jumbotron. The students sing the "Beer Song" while the UW band plays music for it:

In heaven there is no beer, no beer,
but that's why we drink it here, right here
And when we are gone from here,
our friends will be drinking all our beer.

A Wyoming player, after stealing the ball from the other team, sprints to the other end of the court and slam-dunks the ball for two points. Fans cheer loudly.

I feel the thrill of emotion evoked by this basketball event moment. This feat is not easy and does not occur very often, so when it does there is a sizable emotional response.

During the game the coach seems to chew on the referee's ears, yelling and gesticulating. At times the coach's fleeting smile suggests an actor playing up to the crowd. The coach wants the crowd to think he is telling off the referees, but I think he is just conversing with them, maybe trying to mess with their minds. Other times the coach may really be in a rage. The coach has a lot riding on the outcome of the game. There is no explicit gambling on the game by coaches and players, but the coach's contract is full of incentives that pay if certain conditions, like a minimum number of wins, are met. Some fans identify with being the coach and cheer for self vicariously through him. Squatting on the floor, near the sidelines the coach is yelling to the players throughout the entire game during live action. During a full timeout period the coaches huddle separately and then coach meets with the players; during a 30-second timeout the coach goes directly to the players. Timeouts are of different lengths when called by the coach (e.g. full timeouts of 75 seconds or half timeouts of thirty seconds). Other timeouts are either called by players, coaches or referees in the context of the game or by the media, to facilitate advertising on television or radio. (NCAA, 1999, p. 177) So, a break can be taken by the team in possession of the ball with any amount of time left on the clock or by design for media timeouts "after the 16-, 12-, eight- and four-minute marks of each half." (NCAA, 1999, p. 94)

One of the players signals to the crowd to get louder and hopefully distract the other team in their attempt to score. Basketball is supposed to be a no contact sport, but there seems to be enough to justify blowing the whistle at any given time. Sometimes rule violations are called and sometimes they are not. Sometimes referees (refs) 'call the game close' (call everything they see) and other times they 'let them play' (overlook some incidental contact). Fans get mad and upset when there are too many fouls called, interrupting the game. A couple of bad calls during a game can certainly influence the outcome, especially in a close game. The coach gets a technical foul after working the referees a little too hard.

A player for the other team prepares to take a free throw after being fouled. The Jumbotron, located in the shooter's field of vision, displays some bubbly video that is like a liquid giggling. The player makes the first free throw but misses the second one.

When a player from the other team gets his fifth foul and so fouls out of the game, various songs are played, including one with the line "Hit the road Jack and don't you come back no more." Fans enjoy this, and they sing along and yell loudly while watching the dejected player walk to the bench. Even though the player knows he has five fouls, he ignores it and waits for the referees to signal him out. He takes his time exiting. The game resumes.

The coach yells something to the other team's coach, who later said that he never talked to any human being that way. The coaches creep towards each other in front of the scorer's table preparing to lunge towards each other, as if ready to engage in fisticuffs. They are held back by assistant coaches. The other coach signals with his fist for the UW coach to stick it where the sun doesn't shine. Players can get multi-game suspensions if they leave the bench.

Post-Game

The basketball game wraps up as the time on the clock ticks down to zero. Now that the game is over, the UW fight song is played again as the team and the coach shake hands with the other team and coaches. Attendance for the game is provided over the sound system. The radio sports announcers choose and announce the top player of the game.

The entire crowd stays after the game and many—mostly students—storm the floor. This big win requires fans to become part of the game on the floor. Three-fourths of the floor is jam-packed. A ritual is performed as the coach and players take turns cutting off a piece of the net. The players form their circle and jump together. Fans circle around and imitate the players.

As we wait for fans to clear out of the arena, an impatient security person wearing a red jacket asks: "Are you going to leave?" She then points us out to other security as she leaves.

I see the other team's chartered bus exiting the arena after driving up the cement ramp. Eating at a fast food restaurant later I find, to my surprise, players from the other team sharing the role of being just another consumer.

The next day's newspaper shows a picture of eight of the many former great UW players. Incredibly, all of the players shown are white. This is probably due to the matching of story characters to the expected audience reading this particular paper. Left out was a player drafted in the first round of the NBA (Charles Bradley) and assistant coach of the 86-87 team, Anthony Johnson of the 81-82 team, and many others.

Each game gets more exciting as you move from pre-season to regular season to conference games to the conference tournament and then, hopefully, post-season play. Unfortunately, at some point the season will end for UW. One loss ends the season for the team. One win means another game unless the team is now the NCAA or NIT National Champion.

Listening to the post-game talk on the radio, calling in to sports talk radio shows, watching the evening news, reading the next day's newspapers, and surfing the Internet for sports news continue the basketball event. After a fan's team loses and is knocked out of post-season tournaments, some fans will change teams and even wear the logo of the new team along with the logo of the original team. This act facilitates continued 'cheering for self' through identification with a surrogate team.

Practice

When the AA is empty the fan can hear the air circulation fan belts squeak and rattle. Shot clocks on the backboard supports look like ancient rusted iron when they are not powered up. Someone comes in and, while singing, sweeps the floor. When the players arrive, I can hear the basketballs bounce and the tennis shoes squeaking even though I am sitting in row twenty-six to the side of the entry portals.

The coach arrives within seconds of the official practice start time, but after the players are warmed up and all the assistants are in place. Players do not talk during practice unless calling 'ball' on defense and are reprimanded if they transgress. Only assistant coaches directing drills and the coach are allowed to talk. The coach says 'good' hundreds of times during practice. Anytime a player does anything whether they miss a basket or not they get a 'good' from the coach. The number of times he says good in a row before the player's name and the volume represents the degree of "goodness" or the coach's pleasure. I wonder if practice was this pleasant at the beginning of the season.

The basketball event begins for some fans with watching the team practice the week before the game. The practice scrimmage is just like an actual ball game except for the number of fans. About eight fans watch practice while a ball game may have up to sixteen thousand fans. I arrived to watch practice an hour before anyone else was in the AA, after calling ahead to find out when practice would start.

By attending practice my connection and identification with the team, players and even the coach intensified. My perceptions of the coach changed: in practice he is very personable, while during games he seems very intense. Seeing some of the back stage that many fans do not see helped bring home my wearing multiple hats at the same time while in the dual role of a participant (fan) and as an observer (but not for the other team or as a talent scout) doing thesis research.

During practice the coach and players are individually videotaped and interviewed. Later the video will be played on the local news, interviews will be heard on the radio and stories will be run in the local paper. Two UW staff members, an older man and a minority woman, wander throughout the AA repairing seats.

The woman asks me what I am writing down. About eight other fans watch the practice throughout, all middle-aged or older men. Some say "Hi" as they walk by, but do not stop to talk. The UW Sports Information Director walks in from the tunnel and talks to some fans and later talks to the local paper's sports writer down by courtside.

Five or six guards/forwards (players) and four coaches are at one end of court practicing and five or six centers (players) and another four coaches are at the other end of the court. The head coach roams. There is also a weight trainer and a trainer for injuries. The person in charge of academics for basketball athletes does not attend practice. Basically there is one coach per player. However compared to football there are not very many players, and there are over three time as many games, making basketball a more efficient way to get publicity and money for the university.

The coach sends up an assistant coach to find out who I am. The day was colder than usual, so I had on a different coat, sat farther up in the stands to get another perspective, and had on a baseball cap, too, in case this would help with the glare from the artificial lighting. The assistant coach tells me that the coach sent him up here to make sure who I was: "You're from here, right?" "Yes, I'm James a grad student." He then recognizes me and says: "You were in our basketball class." This interesting moment demonstrates my looking at them while being under surveillance at the same time by them. And yet my gaze is not that of just a fan but as a researcher.

Practices are open, but this is the last one before the game. I strategically decide that it might be wise to refrain from further note taking until later, remove my hat, and remove my coat. There is no idle time in practice. Practice is about two hours and is very efficient.

At the end of practice the players shoot high-pressure free throws. Misses mean extra sprints that must be run. Players run "suicides," which start at one end of the court with a sprint to the closest free throw line, back to the start, to half court, back to the start, to the other free throw line, back to the start, to the other end of the court, and back to the start. All must finish in thirty seconds or less. Other sprints are running two back and forth full courts in twenty-two seconds.

This practice is efficient; the players know the drills and only a few seconds elapse between player repetitions. The coach sometimes uses player's names along with good. Very rarely does he say negative things or correct a player. Some players wear white tennis shoes and others have silver ones. Practice is at full speed with an emphasis on quick shooting and defense. A man walks out onto the catwalks high up over the court and fiddles with the lights.

After practice the team is assembled for a team photo. An apparently professional photographer sets up his lights and camera stand. Players are in white uniforms and coaches in black nylon sweats. Hands on knees for those sitting in front, hands behind them for those standing in the back. Tall players and short coaches stand, short players and tall coaches sit. Not allowed in the picture are two coaches (probably graduate assistants) and the two transfer players that must sit out one year before being allowed to play.

All coaches devise a plan for beating their next opponent during the time between games. During the week before a game players practice the tactics. Highly successful coaches often stick with what they believe exploits the opponents weaknesses and emphasizes their own team's strengths. UW's, e.g. Jim Brandenburg, as well as other more famous coaches, like Bobby Knight, winner of three NCAA National Championships, have done great coaching this way. UW's current coach does this too but what makes his style special is the significant adjustments he makes during the game and at halftime. Times of distraction for the fans—timeouts and halftime—are therefore periods of intense concentration for the coach.

Some Identified Patterns

People step into new roles for the basketball event, which transforms them into fans.[11] Students become players and stars. Players become a proxy for those that no longer play basketball, cannot, or never could. Players become representations for fans that identify with the team of players and who share the credit for success and the agony of defeat. Attending a basketball event may be a nice break for Professors who attend them.

Rabid fans may have a hard time stepping into and out of the role of being a fan. Rabid fans may wear their fan cap literally and figuratively all week long. Some casual fans may go to the basketball event just to be part of something big and to see what others do. Fans sometimes get into heated arguments. Some fans, usually inebriated, even engage in fisticuffs.

Those stepping into the role of fan can bask in the glory of the chosen team's success. Once people have stepped into the role of being a fan at a basketball event, their behavior can change. Not only does a fan in essence cheer for self, the fan can get worked up into a frenzy of emotion. Winning is expected, so winning makes the fan feel good that 'we won.' Fans don't say the 'team won' nor do they say, "I won or I lost," but rather speak with collective identities to imagined communities like "we won or they won." Fans say "we" but probably are using the word as a substitute for the word "I." Fans chant 'bullshit' over and over to referees who seem to have made a bad call. Win or lose some teams are singled out for specially caustic abuse like in the repeatedly yelled 'Fuck You, BYU.'

Some fans do wild and crazy things that perhaps they would never otherwise do outside of the basketball event. Fans always seem to choose the local team as their team. While in other parts of culture, people may be jealous, even angry at other people's success or feel smugness at other people's failure, fans take on their team's success as their own success and the team's failure as their own failure. Simply living in the same geographic region provides a collective identity among the residents. Identifying with a team or city seems to attach too much significance to the imagined community. Not only is fan identification with a sport team's success or failure unrealistic so is identifying with a nation or city (e.g. being from Denver but not living there and still feeling connected to it and basking in the regions success).

Fans may be left feeling frustrated and unfulfilled when the team loses. When winning becomes not the question, but by how much, eventually the winning becomes routine and can get boring. Losses over many years, or failing to qualify for the NCAA tournament in over a decade, can make the fans hungry for success.

All fans are there at the pleasure of those who make the basketball event possible. Those in the crowd are easily subjected to surveillance and know that others may be watching them, but are not quite sure if, when, and by whom. At some level, this event is highly structured, even disciplined, despite all its seeming spontaneity. All of those attending the basketball event are easily controlled and are not out causing trouble (i.e. trying to change the way things are). The basketball event is real, is real life and yet is constructed entertainment for fans of a battle that matters only in an imagined sense.[12]

Academic institutions say that your size and physical talent do not matter and that age, race, class, and gender should not matter either, as evidenced in the UW non-discrimination statement. Juxtaposed is the basketball event, where academics do not seem to matter, but physical size and athletic talent do. Here, too, age, race, class, and gender should not matter either. The ideal is noble, but by contrast what goes on in reality reveals another story.

Age, race, class, and gender, (almost without exception) decide what a particular human being can and will do. Look at the roles played by men of means and leisure, as opposed those who lack class status—especially women and minorities. There is little difference between the characters in the academic event and those in the basketball event. White males fill the highest paying roles accompanying the high-class status. The lower-status, lower-paying roles or roles requiring more work, or at least more labor, are filled with lower class types, women, and minorities.

Win or lose, professors and Cowboy Joe Club members can step out of the role of an upper class fan and still have a lot to be thankful for. Despite never having played basketball, or even attending college, some fans still can be part of the basketball event by choosing to buy their way into the Cowboy Joe Club.

Being able to buy in may be the result of enjoying the benefit of profit gleaned from estates or successful ranches built up by ancestors. Athletes may not be academic marvels but they do work and some do get degrees that some fans will never get. Some players and students have in effect bet their very life on success on the court or in the classroom. Fail here, fail now, and stay at the bottom of the class ladder. Work very hard and, with some luck, maybe one will move up the ladder a rung or two.

Some cannot afford to make any mistakes or take any chances in their quest for success while others would actually have to work hard at failing to fail. Those starting out with means and status do not need education in the fight for survival. Life winners and losers go into the basketball event and leave with the same status, whether or not the home team wins the game.

Interestingly, because of the real social distance between fans and participants, players generally do not know the individual fans. Fans learn player names, bios, stats, etc. via the game program, newspapers etc., and start acting and talking as if they really know the players personally, but the players do not know the fans, at least not most of them. It is just a game, but the more you know about the game and the history and the team, the bigger the game becomes. Fans identifying with the team, the coach, and players is a definite pattern found during the basketball event.

People step into the role of fan. Students taking a break from studying go become a fan for a time. Bored state residents become fans during the basketball event as they entertain and are entertained. Some people almost seem to live for the basketball event and the chance to escape reality by moving into the role of a fan and the fantasy of being someone, making a difference, of glory in winning, of being superior to, at least, the other team. For some, it is the only chance during the week to tell others what they think; their exegesis of the actions of characters in the basketball event comes while playing the role of a fan. The referees can be told they are wrong in a loud, offensive, and demeaning manner. If a home team coach loses too many games or cannot get the fans to believe in an unrealistic expectation of greatness, the coach, too, becomes a verbal target of the fans.

Outside of the actual live basketball event, fans may give other fans a hard time if their team loses. Fans may also be razzed when their team does poorly. Fans absorb this verbal abuse and must wait for their team to do better. The other team's players can be taunted in a release of pent-up pain and suffering. Cowboy Joe Club members step into the role of financial elite, fans seeing and being seen. Perhaps they also enjoy seeing and listening to what other fans do and say.

Another pattern is that most team fans believe that their team is the best, however only about forty colleges can claim at least one NCAA basketball championship in all of history, even though there are about three hundred and eighteen division I basketball teams that play the game. The NCAA tournament takes sixty-four teams and the NIT takes thirty-two, so a total of ninety-six teams get post-season play.

Being on the AP top 25-poll list means prime time TV games and wide coverage in the press TV, radio, and papers. Fans brag when they are on the list, but one does not have to look hard to find a team with a better record, that beat even top-25 teams, but is not on the list. Before an AP Poll top 25 ranked team is going to play a game, the fan can look up the point spread (how much a team is expected to win or lose by) in a newspaper. This tells you who is expected to win and by how much. Those that bet on the game often include the point spread, making the deal a fair bet.[13] Betting on a game can make it more exciting, but if you cannot stand to lose, nor afford to lose, it may be better to refrain.

One clear pattern of fan behavior at the basketball event is that of making noise and/or yelling whenever something happens in the game that either they like or dislike i.e. 'cheering for self.' Some fans have a few choice words to yell during the basketball event at referees, cheerleaders, an opposing coach, other fans, and opposing players: Fuck You! BYU, you ain't a gigolo, sit down in front, ref beats his wife, take if off, get off your knee, that's what your wife does for me, cheerleaders just standing, move!, Dumbo cheerleaders why are you here. Hello!, cover the Cowboys, Ugly, they are all ugly, hit him harder: make'em bleed, dive in there scairdy cats, that guy's ugly as hell, kick'em in the groin, you're ugly, c'mon dumb cheerleaders, get off the court fat ass, you suck, come on, tit-for-tat shit, go back to the retirement home, die you little prick die, you suck number 33 you suck, fucking cheaters, start the clock fuck face, fuck you, you suck, bullshit, take it baby, you little homo, little prick ref, bull shit ref, Jesus Christ fucking bullshit, 34 is a fag, son of a bitch, this is fucking bullshit, you suck ref, stupid idiot refs, tall fat faggot, pull your head out you son of a bitch, pop it to em baby, damn this fuckin shit, fucking refs suck bullshit, and damn those bastard refs. The students sing another song that ends with: "we're going to fuckin beat you up."

Fans almost always boo when there is a foul called by a referee on UW. When a bad foul is called on UW, after a shot block and steal, it incites the students to yell while chanting 'bullshit' over and over. Fans identify with the team and take referee penalties against the team personally. Booing is another form of 'cheering for self.' If it was a film, the basketball event could probably get an R rating at worst and a PG-13 at best. When there is no doubt that the call against UW was a good call, fans usually are silent. The BYU Cougars are always singled out for special abuse. Students chant at every opportunity: 'Fuck You, BYU' yelled like a line in a poem. This can be amusing to fans at first, in the attempt to cause BYU to play poorly. After the fact and thinking about it, this is quite rude towards BYU, Utah, and members of the Church of Latter Day Saints. Perhaps the 'black fourteen' incident that was discussed in chapter one and the fact that the BYU team is all white, as is 90% of the audience, provide help explaining the history behind this particular behavior at the UW basketball event.

A basketball event is like a speech. The coach prepares and trains, the team performs the speech or debate on who is better, and fans judge "the speech" subjectively, while the scoreboard judges objectively. The coach must sell the fantasy of an expectation of greatness to the fans. Basketball events provide an opportunity, excuse, or forced interaction of social scripts that are culturally and socially acceptable for people who otherwise would never have contact, let alone interactions.

The coach is selling the fantasy of high expectations. When a coach and team fails by having a losing season, the coach and assistants may have to change schools, but not professions. Getting fired is likely, but not finding similar work is unlikely. The coach, in his first three years, has had two, new upgraded contracts. His current contract, good through 2009, is worth up to over five hundred thousand dollars per year. Coach identifies with the team, as perhaps its biggest fan with the most justified identification, and his yelling and cheering is in fact one of the purest examples of 'cheering for self.'

Money is donated in the name of players of the game to the Cowboy Joe Club. The Cowboy Joe Club in turn provides athletes with scholarships. Theoretically these same dollars could end up benefiting that same player, which seems to skirt the NCAA regulation spirit of players not receiving financial compensation. The Cowboy Joe Club is a non-profit corporation.

Maybe athletic teams should be made up of those possessing an associate degree or of graduate students on stipend. If that was done, people could not say players lack academics, and there would be other sources of money. Academically sound, this could however result in boring basketball events. A key part of college athletics is that the athletes are also college students. The athletes could be paid and not have to be students, too, but this would be too blatant compared to the current fiction.

Compare this to salaries for professors at UW ranging from thirty thousand to one hundred and twenty-five thousand dollars, although some professors can supplement their income through grants, consulting, and publishing. The coach does have to convince teenagers to sign on with the team, a perhaps demeaning duty.[14] His income includes incentives like more pay for selling more tickets. The Cowboy Joe Club supplements his income, too, while the State of Wyoming pays his basic salary. The UW Basketball camp, ads, radio interviews, and the coach's TV show contribute also. Big games on the road boost the coach's bank account too. Most likely, he is the highest paid human being in Wyoming and one of the most well-known publicly. Fans love this coach because he has won a lot of home games. Previous coaches with bad records were severely abused verbally by fans.

One game is really no different from another in physical reality. But I found a difference among games over the season while watching and experiencing many different basketball events. Over the course of the season, feelings tend to increase in intensity. Post-season games are a more powerful experience than pre-season games. Playing a team like Gonzaga during the regular season would just be another game. Playing and beating AP Poll number six-ranked Gonzaga (and an All-American player) in the post-season NCAA tournament on national TV during prime time, especially after so many years since being in the NCAA Tournament, is huge. In fact, some casual fans are more likely to watch a big game than a regular season game. One game is imagined to be huge due to the factors mentioned above, while another visually identical game is relatively boring due to psychic factors alone.

The basketball event is meant to be experienced in real time and few watch game reruns. Hype before a game, increasing identification with the team, having something to lose or gain (i.e. face or respect), the size and intensity of the crowd, the team and its story, and simply learning more and more about the team and the basketball event can change the emotions felt during a basketball event. Increasing identification swells the intensity of emotions evoking 'cheering for self' as evidenced through yelling and booing.

Notes for Chapter Two

[1] Gloria Anzaldua in her book, *Borderlands*, provides a way of looking at borders:
> The actual physical borderland that I'm dealing with in this book is the Texas-U.S., Southwest/Mexican border. The psychological borderlands, the sexual borderlands, the spiritual borderlands are not particular to the Southwest. In fact the Borderlands are physically present wherever two or more cultures edge each other, where people of different races occupy the same territory, where under, lower, middle and upper classes touch, where the space between two individuals shrinks with intimacy. (Anzaldua, 1999, p. 19)

[2] This technique or phenomenon of controlling and designing vantage points is not new and was recognized by Albert Boime in paintings as described in his book *The Magisterial Gaze: Manifest Destiny and American Landscape Painting c. 1830-1865*:
> The privileged nineteenth-century American's experience of the sublime in the landscape occurred on the heights. The characteristic viewpoint of contemporary American landscapists traced a visual trajectory from the uplands to a scenic panorama below. Almost invariably the compositions were arranged with the spectator in mind, either assuming the elevated viewpoint of the onlooker or including a staffage figure seen from behind that functioned as a surrogate onlooker. This Olympian bearing metonymically embraced past, present, and future, synchronically plotting the course of empire. The experience on the heights and its literary and aesthetic translation became assimilated to popular culture and remained and continues to remain a fundamental component of the national dream. As such, it is inseparable from nationalist ideology. I will argue in this essay that there is an American viewpoint in American landscape painting that can be identified with this characteristic line of vision, and that this peculiar gaze represents not only a visual line of sight but an ideological one as well. (Boime, 1991, p. 1-2)

[3] Refer to the Ticket brochure in Appendix 1 that delineates the seating areas or visit the UW web site and click on 'Athletics' then 'tickets' then 'Arena-Auditorium Seating Diagram'. (http://wyomingathletics.fansonly.com/tickets/wyo-hoops-seating.html). For ticket prices and donations to Cowboy Joe Club see 'Men's Basketball Ticket Information: http://wyomingathletics.fansonly.com/tickets/tickets-static-info/tickets-m-basketball.html.

[4] To view a video clip of this game go to: http:/uwadmnweb.uwyo.edu/ahc/digital/qtfiles/NCAA43.MOV.

[5] Note that UW women's basketball games or 'basketball events' are virtually identical to the men's games in spite of there being only a few hundred fans in attendance.

[6] To hear audio play by play and color commentary of a University of Wyoming basketball games go to: http://wyomingathletics.fansonly.com/sports/m-baskbl/sched/wyo-m-baskbl-sched.html. [www.uwyo.edu] (UW, 2002).

[7] To listen to the fight song, go to: http://wyomingathletics.fansonly.com//trads/ragtimecowboyjoe.html.

<u>RAGTIME COWBOY JOE</u>
He always sings
Raggy music to the cattle
as he swings
back and forward in the saddle,
on a horse—a pretty good horse!
He's got a syncopated gaiter,
and you ought to hear the meter
to the roar of his repeater;
how they run—yes run!
When they hear him 'a-comin,'
cause the western folks all know,
he's a high-falootin', rootin, tootin,'
son of a gun from ol' Wyoming,
Ragtime Cowboy
Talk about your Cowboy,
Ragtime Cowboy Joe. (UW, 2002)

[8] According to the Athletic Department no fees are paid since only a small portion of the songs are played. (766-2444)

[9] For more information on the 6th Man Club go to: http://sixthmanclub.net/. (UW, 2002).

[10] Wildfire is managed and supervised by the athletic department. They are all full-time students and get no athletic scholarship aid. The athletic department picks up travel costs. Wildfire members may receive aid from other departments according to the Athletic Department (766-4091).

[11] According to the Oxford English Dictionary a fan is "a keen and regular spectator...a regular supporter...a keen follower." A fanatic is "characterized, influenced, or prompted by excessive and mistaken enthusiasm." A fanatic person is "an unreasoning enthusiast." (Simpson & Weiner, 1989, p. 711-713) Many fans qualify as fanatical fans. The degree of enthusiasm and unreasoning behavior is what seems to separate many fans from the rabid fan.

[12] Michel Foucault in the following passage from his book *Discipline & Punish: The Birth of the Prison* reveals how individuals are produced or fabricated through the process of economic exchange:

> It is often said that the model of a society that has individuals as its constituent elements is borrowed from the abstract juridical forms of contract and exchange...The individual is no doubt the fictitious atom of an 'ideological' representation of society; but he is also a

reality fabricated by this specific technology of power that I have called 'discipline'. We must cease once and for all to describe the effects of power in negative terms: it 'excludes', it 'represses', it 'censors', it 'abstracts', it 'masks', it 'conceals'. In fact, power produces; it produces reality; it produces domains of objects and rituals of truth. The individual and the knowledge that may be gained of him belong to this production. (Foucault, 1977, p. 194)

[13] Bodog.com as of Dec 28, 2001 listed Wyoming as a 100-1 to win the NCAA tournament. (Bodog, 2001).

[14] The concept of the fact that coaches may find recruiting teenagers demeaning was gained through reading John Feinstein's books.

Chapter Three:

An Interpretation and Analysis of the Key Patterns

> This same Round Table series expressed a mistrust of the persuasive power of the advertising. The availability of goods was a sign of national greatness, but too much of a desire for things demonstrated self-indulgence. Goods enticed, and marketing skills coupled with more sophisticated use of media could overwhelm an audience with cash in its pockets. This impatience to buy clouded Americans' feelings of happiness, created a demand for housing that could not be satisfied, and inflected film production toward the facile and the merely entertaining. The American urge to buy immediately and the selling of goods through compelling media presentations had to be contained by a moral leadership that distrusted ephemeral pleasures. (Sandeen, 1995, p. 7)

Concepts[1]

This chapter is an analysis from the view of a detached observer: removing self from the situation and viewing the basketball event from another point located outside of the basketball event. Speaking a language (e.g. English) and reading and writing English helps to construct virtually everyone in a culture into better slaves for society. This is because people in a particular society are only aware of the ways things are and may not have words to describe and discuss other potential ways of living or doing things.

This is similar to removing oneself from orthodoxy and heterodoxy and looking to other ideas. Language provides us with orthodoxy (correct, right "opinion", natural ideas according to those who benefit the most from the way things are), heterodoxy ("wrong opinion", things that we are taught we should not do), and finally doxy or "the aggregate of the 'Choices'" which encompasses both of these, and all of the other ideas that are not even on the radar screen and cannot be thought or discussed because there are no words for them. (Bourdieu, 1994, p. 163,165) People are often given two choices (e.g., you can tell the truth or lie). This leaves out the option of saying nothing at all or a half-truth. Narrowing down people's choices to one or the other and leaving out or discounting all other options like 'neither,' or 'both,' or one of an infinite number of other options is what I mean. This happens especially when the orthodoxy and heterodoxy do not allow for other desired doxa.[2]

Systems of control in basketball events run deeper than the spectator realizes. The experience of attending a basketball event connects the fan to the basketball game and with the advertisers. Without the key phrases "basketball event" and "cheering for self," fans as well as those in academia, cannot articulate and/or recognize the unspoken condition of experiencing a basketball game with the process of consuming advertisers products. Connections yield identifications providing a platform for 'cheering for self.'

Engaging in self-reflexivity is the task at hand. First one can experience the basketball event. Next one can reflect on the basketball event. Self-reflexivity is removing oneself from the reflecting on the basketball event, like imagining seeing yourself looking in a mirror from a point removed from yourself and the mirror.[3]

This thesis is not an exhaustive analysis of the basketball event and it is hoped that the reader will engage the subject.[4] Perhaps attending a basketball event will result in a 'thicker description' or further debate. The American Studies method relies on there being no particular right or wrong answer, but rather by looking very closely at things—by taking an interdisciplinary approach one can get closer to a truth. Hopefully through discussion and debate an element will emerge that helps to explain or understand minutiae within a holistic picture. By examining binary oppositions there may be a way to resolve them or at least to understand them more fully. During the basketball event, the only thing that really matters is the final outcome (i.e. win or lose and the final score).[5] Winning facilitates the ultimate intensity level of fans 'cheering for self.' Events leading up to the game, the actual game, the end of the game, and activities after the game are important too. How you get there is part of the plot. The basketball event script is like formula fiction. The general outline is the same from one game to the next. Knowing the ending makes the event no longer as interesting. "Basketball events" are constructed to be a live event. Once the event is over, there is little interest in listening to the game again or seeing the game again. If fans did become interested in reruns, live basketball events might have less appeal.

For the basketball event, the game begins at a certain time. When the game begins, the game is virtually identical to other games. During the game there is a slow transformation leading up to the break at halftime. Time-outs and referee calls interrupt the evolution of the game for brief periods. Offensive and defensive plays along with called fouls affect the expectation of a particular outcome. Finally the game ends and there is a definite outcome (i.e. win or lose and a degree of winning or losing reflected in the relative scores).

A Brief Narrative Structure or Sequence of the Basketball Event

1. The basketball event is hyped up through various media.
2. The teams warm up and practice on the basketball court.
3. Cowboy fight song is played.
4. Players and coaches are announced.
5. National Anthem is sung.
6. The tip off beginning the game starts at the scheduled time.
7. The game may have lead changes, exciting moments like slam-dunks, and irritants like referees calling fouls on UW.
8. Entertainment takes place during timeouts and halftime.
9. Cotton-Eyed Joe performs.
10. The battle on the floor is resolved via the final score.
11. The win is enjoyed and/or fans look forward to the next game

Another repeated pattern is the basketball event itself. Each basketball event has many common moments that are repeated or that are similar in nature. In *Mastering the crowd: collective behavior and mass society in American social thought, 1917-1939* Leach provides ideas that are easily extended to the basketball event. Having a crowd all concentrating on the flag, on a basketball during a game, and on advertisements helps to construct consumers. "You must fuse your audience or they will not warm to your message." "The crowd intensifies suggestibility" helping to make the individual easier to convince. (Leach, 1986, p. 103) The crowd helps fans to invest in order to connect and identify which in turn supports 'cheering for self.'

The tradition of colleges having basketball events is an old one. Specific traditions are not unique. "Ragtime Cowboy Joe" is a unique fight song, but most teams have a fight song. The basketball event constructs fans to make being a fan a tradition as older fans, perhaps alumni, bring their kids along. Advertisers attempt to make consuming their product a tradition, too. UW hopes fans will consume the intentional collegiate product (the basketball event) and help to sell the college itself to potential attendees as well as alumni. The band member dancing to Cotton-Eyed Joe is a tradition that was recently and spontaneously reinvented.[6] Knowing this, basketball event organizers support traditions and exploit opportunities to fuse audiences and help sustain fans conforming to the process of their own construction by others.

There is a strong pressure for fans to conform, beginning with standing for the National Anthem. Fans are also expected to cheer for UW and to wear UW logo apparel. Many colleges' basketball teams, coaches, players and games are very similar. Familiarity, identification, and loyal dedication make one team preferable and more exciting. Fans can become very excited over a post-season tournament as long as their team is still in it. Once their team loses, the tournament games lose a lot of their appeal for some fans. Some sports fans just enjoy watching sporting events and will follow many teams and many different sports. Some fans bet on games or are members of fantasy sport leagues (a fans fantasy team may include real players from many different real teams and whose weekly real performance affects fantasy game outcomes)—this helps to make e.g. every single NFL game relevant (via connection and identification) to fantasy football league members.[7] These types of fans may watch as many NCAA tournament basketball games as they can regardless of who the teams playing are. Although many games are visually similar, colleges differentiate their product through particular coaches, players, and the college itself. Identification with traditions and acting them out in repetition is another form of 'cheering for self.'

Cheering for Self Explained

Fans with different tastes, class, race, gender, age, education etc. identify with the team if nothing else. This sets the stage for 'cheering for self.' A fan first identifies with something e.g. a product, a team a song, a film clip, an imagined community, or a player. The fan then cheers for positives or against negatives or seeming personal slights. 'Cheering for self' includes making noise by yelling for things they like, booing about things they do not like, displaying logos, and consuming products (the game itself, Pepsi), acting out traditions in repetition, and attending the basketball event due to identification with a team, a coach, a player, a cheerleader, a school, a song, a video clip, a corporation, a product and subsequent action or taking things personally. Although an individual fan would never be missed in reality some fans feel that the team depends on them and they on the team. A fan's team winning facilitates the ultimate 'cheering for self.' Rabid fans crying out with vicious and personal obscenities is the most striking and extreme example of intense identification resulting in 'cheering for self.' The Coach's realistic identification with the team allows his 'cheering for self' (the purest form). Fans identify with the UW product and through attendance at the basketball event are 'cheering for self.'

Loudness Levels

Over a series of basketball events a pattern emerges in the form of a hierarchy of loudness levels representing the emotional intensity for various moments in the basketball event. I gauged the loudness with my own ears, not with any type of scientific instrument.[8] Student fans cheer loudest or first during the Papa John's pizza scream. Next loudest, or second, is when fans yell for Cotton-Eyed Joe while he dances. Next loudest, or third, is when the coach or a player signals with their hands to the fans to get louder. Next loudest, or fourth, is when a player from the other team fouls out. An alley-oop or lobbing the ball to a player near the basket with a slam-dunk or just a slam-dunk is the fifth loudest crowd. A steal with a lay-up is sixth loudest. A technical foul against the other team that means Wyoming gets two free shots and the ball, is the seventh loudest moment. A blocked shot results in approximately the same loudness level, or eighth, as a technical foul. When a Wyoming player steals the ball from the other team is the ninth loudest moment. The tenth loudest moment during a basketball event is when the Cowboys make a three-point shot. A foul called by the referees against Wyoming is usually quite loud, or eleventh. The making of a two-point shot is next, or twelfth, in the hierarchy of loudness. A timeout called by the other team when apparently due to Wyoming scoring a string of unanswered points ranks thirteenth. A long defense that forces the opposing team to use up their shot clock before forcing a shot is fourteenth. Fans chanting 'defense' when the score is too close or UW is behind is fairly loud, or fifteenth. A tie up among players resulting in a jump ball that awards the ball based on alternating possession is sixteenth. The making of a free throw comes up next or seventeenth as far as loudness.

Relative Loudness Levels or hierarchy of Event Moments

1. Papa John's Pizza Scream (loudest)
2. Cotton-Eyed Joe

3. Crowd after the Coach or a player signals for fans to get louder
4. A player from the other team fouls out
5. Alley-oop and slam-dunk or just a slam-dunk
6. A steal followed with a lay-up by Wyoming
7. A technical foul against the other team
8. Blocking a shot by the other team
9. A steal
10. Making a three point shot
11. A foul called on Wyoming
12. A two point shot being made
13. A timeout called by the other team due to UW scoring a series of unanswered points
14. A long defense forcing the other team to use up their shot clock
15. Fans chanting defense when the game is close
16. A tie up among players resulting in a possession change
17. The making of a non-game winning free throw

With each successive moment of success for the home team, the crowd gets increasingly louder. In contrast, one unfavorable moment quiets the crowd all the way back to an initial loudness. When a second moment in a row is one that fans do not like the crowd becomes relatively or completely silent.

The crowd is louder and more excited after a slam-dunk resulting in only two points while a three-point shot elicits less excitement. Assuming the ultimate goal is that your team scores the most points and therefore wins, this is nonsensical. Each time a good moment in the game occurs, without a bad moment like a missed shot, the crowd gets louder and louder.

The fan is constantly bombarded with noise throughout the event. A fan almost never hears silence or conversation from afar. Fans receive input mostly in the form of seeing the teams playing on the court (not counting noise produced by other fans, referee's whistles, game horns etc). Fan output is mostly noise produced via yelling and some body language. Players communicate by their physical actions and get input from the crowd through hearing the noise produced by fans. Fans want to yell or boo to express verbally with noise their cheering for self.

When a rabid fans yells out something, it is one of the quietest moments during the basketball event in relative terms. For those within earshot, the words that are yelled by a single rabid fan ring out and are intelligible. Rabid fans usually yell before or after the crowd. Since other fans are usually quiet when rabid fans are yelling, the rabid fans' comments are perhaps more noticeable than all of the other loudness levels.

This is the most striking example of a fan cheering for self i.e. rabid fans yelling out. Other fans do not overly identify with other fans and feel responsible for them. If a player or coach or advertiser yelled out obscenities with the same personal viciousness they would suffer due to social pressure and consequences arising from fans identifying with them and not wanting to be associated with them when they act like that. Other fans are heard but are ignored for the most part, as they are not the point of visual and psychic attention for those who are not fans of fans.

Mostly men do the yelling of obscenities, but women sometimes make similar comments. Typically two or three loud and obnoxious fans within earshot are responsible for yelling all of the obscenities heard during the course of a basketball event. Further study could perhaps be done by interviewing rabid fans after the game or after the season is over.

During the basketball event, fans and others seem to ignore, tune-out or, in some cases, enjoy the outbursts by rabid fans. No one seems offended by the remarks. No one chastises or expresses dissatisfaction or no one feels comfortable enough to complain. Many students probably simply do not care. At some pro sporting events, if you cuss you are removed. This may not be true at UW because students get in free and the students presence is highly desired by the institution while at pro sporting events individual fans who are annoying are easily replaced while other paying fans can then be retained.

Until I started to really pay attention and record the remarks I had no idea how many statements are made and just how obscene they are. Fans often hear, but let go, and soon forget, yelled comments made by rabid fans. During the basketball event they seem appropriate for those in the role of a fan.

However when one revisits and looks at yelled comments outside the context of the basketball event, they no longer seem so tame. If someone yelled these things during a class or other public setting, there would be serious consequences. During a game the obnoxious fan is on the public stage, but is mostly anonymous, with only a few fans seeing who they are. Other fans may be distracted by the game and have strong emotions that cause them to feel like yelling, too. Silent fans may have some agreement with the sentiments in general and while caught up in the game they do not dwell upon the yelled remarks.

Advertising: Ads are Everywhere to be Seen, Heard, and Experienced

Potential advertising provides a strong incentive for constructing and supporting certain large crowds accompanying the predetermined basketball event. On the other hand, crowds of people formed to protest something are broken up. Corporations, UW, and fans do not care why there is a crowd, only that there is one. Fans are provided with the suspense of not knowing for sure who will win, but few or no surprises occur.

The pervasiveness and continuity of ads throughout the duration of the basketball event is remarkable. There is a pattern throughout basketball events of bombarding fans with as many ads as possible. From the beginning, newspapers, pre-game on the radio, the game program, post game on the radio and Cowboy Talk, the evening news on TV, newspapers the day after and the Internet all display ads to be seen, heard, and experienced. Those listening to the game on the radio can be bombarded with five to ten minutes of ads after the teaser that the announcers will be back to wrap things up momentarily. Wrapping things up can be just signing off. Forty minutes of game time (which can be seen as an ad for UW, at some level) seems to be a distraction and barely fits in between two hours of corporate ads. Corporations hope fans will identify with products and cheer for self in that identification through the consumption of their products. Corporations thereby cheer for self too. Ads, logos, and donating money are examples of corporations cheering for self during the basketball event.

There are several different media types used to present ads. UW uses the team, including players and coaches, as one form of media to advertise UW. Another media form includes the walking slice of pizza. The pizza scream and giving out some free pizza is one way to get people to hear about and buy their pizza. The loudspeakers blast audio of commercials to the mass audience who will hear the ads unless they are wearing earplugs or are listening to the game on the radio with a headset. Logos, symbols, and ads are plastered all over the AA. (Refer to Appendix 2 for a listing of some logos, words, and phrases observed at basketball events.)

On the court, on chairs, on scoreboards, and above entry portals textual ads and logos abound. Ads appear on drink cups from the concession stand and throughout game programs. The Jumbotron is used for video ads. Fans wearing UW apparel and 6th Man Club shirts act as advertising media for products, including UW.

Many students are not old enough to consume alcohol legally and while radio ads during the basketball event discourage the use of alcohol, radio ads also bombard fans, encouraging the purchase of alcoholic beverages. The same basketball event seems to be both for and against alcohol. A walking slice of Papa John's Pizza is the only de facto mascot seen during basketball events. There are so many ads because the network has to recoup the broadcast rights. The ads are completely invasive with their non-stop frequency and rapid pace. In February 1999 ESPN agreed to pay $48 million over seven years to broadcast Mountain West Conference football and basketball. (Media Guide, 2000-2001, p. 135) It should come as no surprise that the university's schedule is at the command of this cable television network. Tip off time can be as late as 10:00 p.m. to fit into the network's schedule. Monday night is most susceptible to this manipulation. The balance of the schedule can take up any of the other nights of the week except Tuesday, which did not have any basketball events this season.

Having everyone in the arena concentrating and focusing on the basketball and UW's product (the team) helps condition people to pay attention. Later, when other advertisers have their time to try and capture the audience they are much more successful. The fans are in place and do not want to miss the rest of the basketball event, so they are not going to be offended and walk off when bombarded with ads. Fans cannot hit the mute button or leave the room. They can get bored fast and want to be entertained by the game and barring that, why not an advertisement? The entire basketball event including the game itself is nothing but advertisement. Even fans sitting in the Cowboy Joe Club seating areas are advertising themselves to others.

The University of Wyoming athletic department has even done a study via survey to try and identify what fans really want, including game start times and loudness levels of songs. This is no different than the market research corporations do with regard to their products.

Managers of the game manipulate—but also respond to—fan loudness. Fans are constructed by the basketball event to identify with the team and to become more fan-like. The basketball event has varying loudness levels. The loudness and intensity can increase up to a peak and then drop off. There is a certain rhythm or cadence in the varying loudness levels between quiet and very loud. There are lots of ups and downs during the game. The intensity of loudness and emotion varies in intensity and between pleasant emotions and irritating emotions. There are periods of intense involvement by fans, followed by periods of relaxation.

The basketball event experience teaches fans to be consumers of the game and of advertisers products. There is a parallel between wanting to drink a Pepsi due to thirst, acquiring a Pepsi, drinking a Pepsi, and relaxing with satisfaction and wanting to see your team score, seeing your team score, and relaxing with satisfaction. There is a direct example or connection between experiencing the basketball event and consuming products: when the team, with whom the fans identify, scores three points, a free t-shirt is thrown into the crowd!

Fans consume the basketball event and the game itself. Fans are taught to consume a particular product like Pepsi and a particular team. Fans learn what to expect from the team and from certain products. Fans become familiar with the coach and the team players as well as with brand names of products. Fans may misidentify game emotion and excitement with particular products. Fans become intensely loyal to the UW product—the team—just as fans become loyal consumers of certain other brands of products. UW is selling the product consisting of the team and the basketball event. Consuming advertisers products is a form of cheering for self as the fan identifies with the corporation and products.

Fans identify with the team, products, and UW and so when they cheer they are in fact "cheering for self." Fans are constructed by the basketball event to be fans and consumers. A fan's self is constructed/made by the basketball event. Rabid fans help to make new attendees into fans and advertising helps make one a better consumer of the "right" products. The entire basketball event is interwoven with fans "cheering for self" and advertisers (including UW) trying sell their products. All of those present at the basketball event are connected through it. The basketball event, through "cheering for self," teaches one to be a fan, a consumer of UW's basketball games, and the buyer of products of advertisers.

This understanding of the basketball event in general is shaped by similarities found among a number of specific basketball events. Converting fan behaviors, like yelling, from fan language into words on pages that interpret or explain them is accomplished by translating them into terms and concepts that non-fans can relate to. Fans "cheering for self" during the basketball event seems to indirectly explain their motivation and behavior, while at the same time suggesting that fans are constructed to be fans, to consume a UW product—the basketball event, and to be consumers of advertisers' products.

Claude Levi-Strauss in his book *Myth and Meaning: Cracking the Code of Culture* provides some relevant insight:

> it is the quest for the invariant, or for the invariant elements among superficial differences. The problem…is also to try to understand what is invariant in the tremendous diversity of landscapes, that is, to be able to reduce a landscape to a finite number of…layers…to try to reach the invariant property of a very complex set of codes…The problem is to find what is common to all of them. It's a problem, one might say, of translation, of translating what is expressed in one language—or one code, if you prefer, but language is sufficient—into expression in a different language. (Levi-Strauss, 1978, pp. 8-9)

Put in the context of basketball, this means reducing the fan experience during 'basketball events' to a few common elements. One key underlying element is that of 'cheering for self.' This thesis has attempted to explain how the "invariant" aspect of fans "cheering for self" in the 'basketball event' is related to many facets—like advertising—at several levels. Although the 'basketball event' experience is complex and seemingly chaotic on the surface, there are definite patterns that reveal active construction of fans—through 'cheering for self'—into consumers of basketball games and commercial products during 'basketball events.'

Notes for Chapter Three

[1] Literature Review

One can view the film "Blue Chips" to get a feel for the pressures facing a coach during recruiting while dealing with NCAA regulations. The film "Hoosiers" provides a sense of the excitement of the game of basketball.

There are a number of good books by sports journalists that provide insights about college basketball. These include John Feinstein, Billy Packer, and H.G. Bissinger. John Feinstein's basketball books look into various aspects of the game, and give a feeling for ways to look at it. In *A Season Inside: One Year in College Basketball*, he looked at basketball in totality. Feinstein went to practices, private meetings, and events, learning about the personal lives of the various characters (players, coaches, referees etc.) and what they are thinking during an entire season. He interacted closely, including question and answer sessions, and even traveled with teams. Recruiting and signing players may mean ensuring that when athletes visit a campus they get taken to the right parties. Feinstein states: "Rarely does a player choose a school simply because he believes it will be the best place for him athletically and academically" (Feinstein, 1988, p31).

In *Forever's Team: The Story of the 1977-1978 Duke University Basketball Team*, Feinstein follows the players on a team that went from the bottom of their conference to almost winning a national title. He follows their lives over many years from before college, during college, and after college. He emphasizes basketball and life's related ups and downs. "Duke students clearly looked upon basketball as a participation—not a spectator—sport." (Feinstein, 1990, p. 20-1)

In the book *A Season on the Brink: A Year with Bobby Knight and the Indiana Hoosiers*, Feinstein talks about the Indiana Hoosiers. During one season, Feinstein studies Head Coach Bobby Knight's personality and interaction with the team. Feinstein had inside access to everything the coach and team did that was directly related to basketball. Feinstein explains that "Players are given cars, money…you name it, and the NCAA almost never proves anything." (Feinstein, 1989, p119)

In *The Last Amateurs: Playing for Glory and Honor in Division I College Basketball*, Feinstein suggests that virtually all college basketball teams are no longer amateurs playing ball while getting an education. The Patriot league was formed to provide the Ivy League with non-conference football games. "They didn't want to play too far 'up'—and have their players beaten to a pulp by teams that averaged 300 pounds a man across the offensive line…[and follows the] Ivy League model: no athletic scholarships." (Feinstein, 2000, p. 14-15)

In preparing to write *A March to Madness: The View from the Floor in the Atlantic Coast Conference*, Feinstein was allowed into many aspects of coaches' and players' worlds for most of the teams in one conference for one season. Feinstein talks about all the pressure and the madness of March created by the NCAA basketball tournament.

Billy Packer, in his book for the general public, talks about being a sports announcer and refers to the world famous sports announcer from Wyoming, Kurt Gowdy, as "the crème de la crème of broadcasting." (Packer & Lazenby, 1985, p. 76) *HOOPS! Confessions of a College Basketball Analyst* is an interesting and captivating quick read.

H.G. Bissinger, in *Friday Night Lights: A Town, a Team, and a Dream,* talks about the culture of high school football in a small town.

> A variety of names came up, but all roads led to West Texas, to a town called Odessa. It was in the severely depressed belly of the Texas oil patch, with a team in town called the Permian Panthers that played to as many as twenty thousand fans on a Friday night. (Bissinger, 1990, p. xi)

Bissinger discusses how the players represent the town and football is everything. This story emphasizes an ugly side of sports.

[2] Michael Frisch in his *Portraits in Steel* talks about people answering 'both' or 'neither' to either/or questions. (Frisch, 1993)

[3] Although referring to globalization, Mergan's text eloquently describes crucial concepts used in this study to look at culture.

> American studies will be most useful to understanding globalization if it maintains its historic purpose of describing, comparing, and explaining the core of the national culture of the United States. Retaining this focus does not mean acceptance of old myths or endorsement of the status quo; rather, it is a challenge to do better with our proven tools—**interdisciplinarity, self-reflexivity, and holism.** [emphasis added] While the interrelations of racial, ethnic, class, gender, generational, and regional identities and cultures are part of the fascinating fabric of all cultures, they exist in political and territorial entities called nations and share laws, rituals, and history. Each unit, local and national, ascribed or chosen, has borders that ultimately link all nations of the globe. (Mergen, 2000, p. 315)

[4] Abraham Cohen in his book *Everyman's Talmud: The Major Teachings of the Rabbinic Sages* talks about the Talmudic argument that is similar to the American Studies method. Whether the subject is basketball, or, as Cohen describes, sacred texts; there is understanding at a higher level to be gained.

> A dialectical inquiry made up of questions and answers, yielding propositions and counterarguments...not a finished statement but notes toward the main points of an argument. These notes permit us to reconstruct the issues and the questions, the facts and the use made of those facts, with the result that when we grasp the document, we also enter into its discipline and join in its argument. (Cohen, 1949, p. x)

[5] Janice Radway's *Reading the Romance: Women, Patriarchy, and Popular Literature* explains how important the ending moment is to those that read romance novels. Sometimes many pages are skimmed or skipped in order to find out how the relationship is consummated. Apparently once enough is read to emphasize suspense, then the moment can occur. Suspense is a key required element, while simple surprise violates the readers' genre expectations. As soon as the ending is known then the novel no longer holds much interest.

> When Vladimir Propp's method for determining the essential narrative structure of folktales is applied to these particular novels, it becomes clear that despite individual and isolated preoccupation with such things as reincarnation, adultery, amnesia, and mistaken identity, these stories are all built upon a shared narrative structure. Assuming first, as Will Wright does, that all narratives are composed of three essential stages—an initial situation, a final transformation of that situation, and an intermediary intervention that causes and explains the change—I then proceeded by trying to identify the common opening and the conclusion of the romances in question. (Radway, 1984, p. 133-4)

Sporting events are no different.

6 Eric Hobsbawm in his book *The Invention of Tradition* provides a definition for 'invented traditions:'

> The term 'invented tradition' is used in a broad, but not imprecise sense. It includes both 'traditions' actually invented, constructed and formally instituted and those emerging in a less easily traceable manner within a brief and dateable period—a matter of a few years perhaps—and establishing themselves with great rapidity. (Hobsbawm & Ranger, 1983, p. 1)

7 There are fantasy leagues for many sports including football, baseball, and basketball. Winning a fantasy league usually means winning money along with the respect and admiration (or contempt) of fellow league members as well as fantasy post-season play. Fantasy league members may meet in member homes to draft players before the season starts, get weekly e-mails of results, and can buy, sell, or trade players. Fantasy league members act as the teams owner, coach, scout etc. Fantasy leagues attempt to parallel or mimic real sports leagues in every way possible. Some leagues allow fantasy team owners to retain their fantasy players from season to season. There are even magazines dedicated to helping readers draft the best players for their fantasy team. Of course all traditional sports media on the real sport provide good information for fantasy league participants. Each week the starters are chosen by a fantasy team's owner from the available fantasy team players that are on that particular fantasy team.

8 The ranking of the relative loudness of event moments was measured qualitatively by my ears and not quantitatively with noise meters. Even so, technically TV commercials watched at home are scientifically said to be the same loudness as the regular programming even though most people have noticed that commercials seem much louder.

Having relied heavily on hearing as opposed to vision throughout life I believe my rankings from the loudest to the quietest have some merit in spite of being my own personal opinion. As a test I looked at moment number seventeen and compared this to moment sixteen while working my way up from the quietest moment to the loudest moment. This test did not result in changes being required. The relative loudness levels were compared over all of the home games during an entire season. Even though other fans might rank the events differently if they were to be surveyed I suspect that the general relative order would be quite similar.

APPENDIX 1: TICKET BROCHURES AND SCHEDULE

APPENDIX 2: LIST OF LOGOS, WORDS, AND PHRASES OBSERVED AT BASKETBALL EVENTS

6th Man Club (shirt says AND 1, Brown and Gold, Pepsi, and Mix 105.5)
AND 1 Basketball
Brown and Gold
Bud Light
Casper Star Tribune
CBS 5
CellularOne
Cheyenne Frontier Days
Coach Steve McClain
Comfort Inn
Community First Insurance
Conoco
Corral West
Country Supermarket Liquors
Cowboy Glass
Cowboy Joe Club
Cowboy Joe Scholarship Fund
ESPN
FBC
Film phrases and screen celebrities
    Tommy Boy, Patton, Happy Gilmore; Belushi—it ain't over till we say its over: when the going gets tough the tough get going
Ford
Gatorade
Gem City Bone and Joint
High Country Stoves
Holiday Inn
Ikia
Ikon
Kinder-Morgan gas stoves
KOWB 1290-Sports Announcer

Cheering For Self

Laramie Daily Boomerang-Sports Writer
Laramie GM Auto
Laramie Lumber
McDonalds
Library Bar and Restaurant
Mini-Mart
Mix FM 105.5
Modern Printing
Mountain Cement
Mountain Standard Time clock
Mountain West Conference
Mullens Heating
OCI
Outback Steak House
Papa John's Pizza
Pepsi
Pilot Wendys
Players (they advertise themselves to the NBA with their name & UW with Wyoming on the front of their shirt)
Pugh Trash Removal
Qwest
RAG Coal West
Reserve Officer Training Corps
Rocky Mountain Ford
Songs: 'Cotton-Eyed Joe,' 'YMCA,' 'Who Let the Dogs Out,' 'Twist and Shout,' 'National Anthem,' 'rap,' 'rock'n roll,' 'country,' 'UW fight song,' student 'Beer song.
State Farm
Super 8
CBS 5, ESPN, Cheers
Thunder Basin Coal Mine
University of Wyoming Sports Information Director
University of Wyoming
Uniwyo
U.S. Flag
Verizon
Village Inn
Wingers
Wyomingathletics.com
Wyoming Cowboys

Wyoming Flag
Wyoming Mining Association
Wyoming Student Loan Corporation
Wyoming Trona Production on Perspective

REFERENCE BIBLIOGRAPHY

American Heritage Center (AHC) (2002). BLACK14.MOV. Retrieved April 24, 2002 from the World Wide Web: http://uwadmnweb.uwyo.edu/ahc/digital/qtfiles/BLACK14.mov

American Heritage Center (AHC) (2002). NCAA43.MOV. Retrieved April 25, 2002 from the World Wide Web: http://uwadmnweb.uwyo.edu/ahc/digital/qtfiles/NCAA43.MOV

Anderson, B. (1983). Imagined Communities: Reflections on the Origin and Spread of Nationalism. New York: Verso Press. ISBN: 0-86091-546-8.

Anzaldua, G. (1999). Borderlands (2nd ed.). San Francisco: Aunt Lute Books.

Bacon-Smith, C. (1992). Enterprising Women: Television Fandom and the Creation of Popular Myth. Philadelphia: University of Pennsylvania Press.

Bissinger, H. (1990). FRIDAY NIGHT LIGHTS: A Town, a Team, and a Dream. Reading, MA: Addison-Wesley Publishing Company, Inc.

Bodog (2001). Bodog. Retrieved December 28, 2001 from the World Wide Web: http://www.bodog.com

Boime, A. (1991). The Magisterial Gaze: Manifest Destiny and American Landscape Painting c. 1830-1865. Washington D.C.: Smithsonian Institution Press.

Bourdieu, P. (1994). Structures, Habitus, Power: Basis for a Theory of Symbolic Power, Doxa, Orthodoxy, and Heterodoxy. In Dirks, N., Eley, G., Ortner, S. (Ed.), Culture/Power/History: A Reader in Contemporary Social Theory (p. Chpt 4). Unk: Princeton U. Press.

Cohen, A. (1949). Everyman's Talmud: The Major Teachings of the Rabbinic Sages. New York: Schocken Books.

Dorst, J. (1999). Looking West. Philadelphia: University of Pennsylvania Press.

Feinstein, J. (1988). A Season Inside: One Year in College Basketball. New York: Villard Books.

Feinstein, J. (1989). A Season on the Brink: A Year with Bobby Knight and the Indiana Hoosiers. New York: A Fireside Book by Simon and Schuster Trade.

Feinstein, J. (1990). Forever's Team: The Story of the 1977-1978 Duke University Basketball Team. New York: Simon & Schuster Trade Paperbacks.

Feinstein, J. (1998). A March to Madness: The View from the Floor in the Atlantic Coast Conference. New York: Little, Brown & Company.

Feinstein, J. (2000). The Last Amateurs: Playing for Glory and Honor in Division I College Basketball. New York: Little Brown and Company.
Foucault, M. (1977). Discipline and Punish: The Birth of the Prison. New York: Pantheon Books. ISBN: 0-394-49942-5
Frisch, M. (1993). Portraits in Steel. Ithaca, NY: Cornell University Press.
Geertz, C. (1973). Thick Description: Toward an Interpretive Theory of Culutre. In (Ed.), The Interpretation of Cultures (2000 Edition ed., pp. 3-30). New York: Basic Books.
Hayden, D. (1995). The Power of Place: Urban Landscapes as Public History. Cambridge, MA: The MIT Press. ISBN: 0-262-58152-3.
Hobsbawm, E., Ranger, T. (Ed.). (1983). The Invention of Tradition. New York: Cambridge University Press.
Hoosiers (HBO Video). (1986). United States: HBO Video.
Larson, T. (1978). The History of Wyoming (2nd ed.). Lincoln, NE: University of Nebraska Press.
Leach, E. (1986). mastering the crowd: collective behavior and mass society in American social thought, 1917-1939. American Studies, 27(Vol 1), 99-114. ISSN: 0026-3079. Coe Ref: E 169.1.M6215 v.27-28.
Levi-Strauss, C. (1978). Myth and Meaning: Cracking the Code of Culture. New York: Schocken Books. ISBN: 0-8052-1038-5.
Mergen, B. (2000). Globalization, Transnationalism, and the End of the American Century: Can American Studies be Globalized? American Studies, Summer/Fall 2000(41:2/3), 303-320.
NCAA (1999). 2000 Official Rules of Basketball. Chicago: Triumph Books.
Packer, B., Lazenby, R. (1985). HOOPS! Confessions of a College Basketball Analyst. Chicago: Contemporary Books, Inc.
Pitcher, G. (2001). McFadden: The Town They Called "Camp". Unk: Goldie Norah Pitcher.
Radway, J. (1984). Reading the Romance: Women, Patriarchy, and Popular Literature. Chapel Hill, NC: The University of North Carolina Press. ISBN: 0-8078-4349-0.
Rappaport, M. (Producer) (1994). Blue Chips. United States: Paramount Pictures.
Sandeen, E. (1995). Picturing an Exhibition: The Family of Man and 1950's America. Albuquerque: University of New Mexico Press.
Simpson, J., Weiner, E. (1989). Oxford English Dictionary (2nd ed.). New York: Clarendon Press. V.5. Coe Ref PE 1625.087 1989.
Spindel, C. (2000). Dancing at Halftime: Sports and the Controversy over American Indian Mascots. New York: New York University Press.
Thoreau, D. (1849). Civil Disobedience. New York: Dover Publications, Inc..

University of Wyoming (2002). UW. Retrieved April 9, 2002 from the World Wide Web: http://www.uwyo.edu

UW (2002). Ragtime Cowboy Joe. Retrieved January 16, 2002 from the World Wide Web: http://wyomingathletics.fansonly.com//trads/ragtimecowboyjoe.html

UW (2002). Sixth Man Club. Retrieved December 18, 2002 from the World Wide Web: http://sixthmanclub.net/

UW (2002). Wyoming Athletics. Retrieved March 9, 2002 from the World Wide Web: http://wyomingathletics.fansonly.com/boosters/boosters-static-info/booster-overview.html

UW (2002). Wyoming Mens Basetball Schedule. Retrieved Febuary, 25, 2002 from the World Wide Web: http://wyomingathletics.fansonly.com/sports/m-baskbl/sched/wyo-m-baskbl-sched.html

Veblen, T. (1998). The Theory of the Leisure Class. New York: Prometheus Books.

REFERENCES

Abbey, Beverly. (2000). Instructional and Cognitive Impacts of Web-Based Education. Hershey, PA: Idea Group Publishing. Coe Libr. Call #: LB 1044.87.I545 2000. ISBN: 1-878-28959-4.

Abel, R. (Ed.). (1995). The Law & Society Reader. New York: New York University Press.

Abrams, M.H. (1988). A Glossary of Literary Terms (5th ed.). Orlando, FL: Holt, Rinehart, & Winston, Inc.

Adams, L., Teall, E., & Taylor, C.R. (Eds.). (1951). Webster's Illustrated Dictionary. New York: Books, Inc.

Adams, S. (1993). Dogbert's Clues for the Clueless. Kansas City, KS: Andrews and McMeel. ISBN: 0-8362-1737-3.

Adams, S. (1996). The Dilbert Principle. New York: HarperBusiness. ISBN: 0-88730-787-6.

Adleman, R., & Walton, G. (1966). The Devil's Brigade. New York: Bantam Books.

Adler, M., & Van Doren, C. (1972). How to Read a Book. New York: MJF Books. ISBN: 1-56731-010-9.

Adler, M.J. (2000). How to Think about the Great Ideas: From the Great Books of Western Civilization. Weismann, M., (Ed.). Chicago, IL: Open Court. ISBN: 0-8126-9412-0.

Adler, M.J. (Ed. in Chief). (1952). Great Books of the Western World: The Great Conversation. (Vol. 1). Chicago, IL: Encyclopedia Britannica, Inc.

Adler, M.J. (Ed. in Chief). (1952). Great Books of the Western World: The Great Ideas: A Syntopican I: Angel to Love. (Vol. 2). Chicago, IL: Encyclopedia Britannica, Inc.

Adler, M.J. (Ed. in Chief). (1952). Great Books of the Western World: The Great Ideas: A Syntopican II: Man to World. (Vol. 3). Chicago, IL: Encyclopedia Britannica, Inc.

Adler, M.J. (Ed. in Chief). (1952). Great Books of the Western World: The Iliad of Homer/The Odyssey. (Vol. 4). Chicago, IL: Encyclopedia Britannica, Inc.

Adler, M.J. (Ed. in Chief). (1952). Great Books of the Western World: Aeschylus, Sophocles, Euripides, & Aristophanes. (Vol. 5). Chicago, IL: Encyclopedia Britannica, Inc.

Adler, M.J. (Ed. in Chief). (1952). Great Books of the Western World: Herodotus & Thucydides. (Vol. 6). Chicago, IL: Encyclopedia Britannica, Inc.

Adler, M.J. (Ed. in Chief). (1952). Great Books of the Western World: Plato. (Vol. 7). Chicago, IL: Encyclopedia Britannica, Inc.

Adler, M.J. (Ed. in Chief). (1952). Great Books of the Western World: Aristotle I. (Vol. 8). Chicago, IL: Encyclopedia Britannica, Inc.

Adler, M.J. (Ed. in Chief). (1952). Great Books of the Western World: Aristotle II. (Vol. 9). Chicago, IL: Encyclopedia Britannica, Inc.

Adler, M.J. (Ed. in Chief). (1952). Great Books of the Western World: Hippocrates & Galen. (Vol. 10). Chicago, IL: Encyclopedia Britannica, Inc.

Adler, M.J. (Ed. in Chief). (1952). Great Books of the Western World: Euclid, Archimedes, Apollonius of Perga, & Nicomachus. (Vol. 11). Chicago, IL: Encyclopedia Britannica, Inc.

Adler, M.J. (Ed. in Chief). (1952). Great Books of the Western World: Lucretius, Epictetus, & Marcus Aurelius. (Vol. 12). Chicago, IL: Encyclopedia Britannica, Inc.

Adler, M.J. (Ed. in Chief). (1952). Great Books of the Western World: Virgil. (Vol. 13). Chicago, IL: Encyclopedia Britannica, Inc.

Adler, M.J. (Ed. in Chief). (1952). Great Books of the Western World: Plutarch. (Vol. 14). Chicago, IL: Encyclopedia Britannica, Inc.

Adler, M.J. (Ed. in Chief). (1952). Great Books of the Western World: Tacitus. (Vol. 15). Chicago, IL: Encyclopedia Britannica, Inc.

Adler, M.J. (Ed. in Chief). (1952). Great Books of the Western World: Ptolemy, Copernicus, & Kepler. (Vol. 16). Chicago, IL: Encyclopedia Britannica, Inc.

Adler, M.J. (Ed. in Chief). (1952). Great Books of the Western World: Plotinus. (Vol. 17). Chicago, IL: Encyclopedia Britannica, Inc.

Adler, M.J. (Ed. in Chief). (1952). Great Books of the Western World: Augustine. (Vol. 18). Chicago, IL: Encyclopedia Britannica, Inc.

Adler, M.J. (Ed. in Chief). (1952). Great Books of the Western World: Thomas Aquinas I. (Vol. 19). Chicago, IL: Encyclopedia Britannica, Inc.

Adler, M.J. (Ed. in Chief). (1952). Great Books of the Western World: Thomas Aquinas II. (Vol. 20). Chicago, IL: Encyclopedia Britannica, Inc.

Adler, M.J. (Ed. in Chief). (1952). Great Books of the Western World: Dante. (Vol. 21). Chicago, IL: Encyclopedia Britannica, Inc.

Adler, M.J. (Ed. in Chief). (1952). Great Books of the Western World: Chaucer. (Vol. 22). Chicago, IL: Encyclopedia Britannica, Inc.

Adler, M.J. (Ed. in Chief). (1952). Great Books of the Western World: Machiavelli, & Hobbes. (Vol. 23). Chicago, IL: Encyclopedia Britannica, Inc.

Adler, M.J. (Ed. in Chief). (1952). Great Books of the Western World: Rabelais. (Vol. 24). Chicago, IL: Encyclopedia Britannica, Inc.

Adler, M.J. (Ed. in Chief). (1952). Great Books of the Western World: Montaigne. (Vol. 25). Chicago, IL: Encyclopedia Britannica, Inc.

Adler, M.J. (Ed. in Chief). (1952). Great Books of the Western World: Shakespeare I. (Vol. 26). Chicago, IL: Encyclopedia Britannica, Inc.

Adler, M.J. (Ed. in Chief). (1952). Great Books of the Western World: Shakespeare II. (Vol. 27). Chicago, IL: Encyclopedia Britannica, Inc.

Adler, M.J. (Ed. in Chief). (1952). Great Books of the Western World: Gilbert, Galileo, & Harvey. (Vol. 28). Chicago, IL: Encyclopedia Britannica, Inc.

Adler, M.J. (Ed. in Chief). (1952). Great Books of the Western World: Cervantes. (Vol. 29). Chicago, IL: Encyclopedia Britannica, Inc.

Adler, M.J. (Ed. in Chief). (1952). Great Books of the Western World: Francis Bacon. (Vol. 30). Chicago, IL: Encyclopedia Britannica, Inc.

Adler, M.J. (Ed. in Chief). (1952). Great Books of the Western World: Descartes & Spinoza. (Vol. 31). Chicago, IL: Encyclopedia Britannica, Inc.

Adler, M.J. (Ed. in Chief). (1952). Great Books of the Western World: Milton. (Vol. 32). Chicago, IL: Encyclopedia Britannica, Inc.

Adler, M.J. (Ed. in Chief). (1952). Great Books of the Western World: Pascal. (Vol. 33). Chicago, IL: Encyclopedia Britannica, Inc.

Adler, M.J. (Ed. in Chief). (1952). Great Books of the Western World: Newton & Huygens. (Vol. 34). Chicago, IL: Encyclopedia Britannica, Inc.

Adler, M.J. (Ed. in Chief). (1952). Great Books of the Western World: Locke, Berkeley, & Hume. (Vol. 35). Chicago, IL: Encyclopedia Britannica, Inc.

Adler, M.J. (Ed. in Chief). (1952). Great Books of the Western World: Swift & Sterne. (Vol. 36). Chicago, IL: Encyclopedia Britannica, Inc.

Adler, M.J. (Ed. in Chief). (1952). Great Books of the Western World: Fielding. (Vol. 37). Chicago, IL: Encyclopedia Britannica, Inc.

Adler, M.J. (Ed. in Chief). (1952). Great Books of the Western World: Montesquieu & Rousseau. (Vol. 38). Chicago, IL: Encyclopedia Britannica, Inc.

Adler, M.J. (Ed. in Chief). (1952). Great Books of the Western World: Adam Smith. (Vol. 39). Chicago, IL: Encyclopedia Britannica, Inc.

Adler, M.J. (Ed. in Chief). (1952). Great Books of the Western World: Gibbon I. (Vol. 40). Chicago, IL: Encyclopedia Britannica, Inc.

Adler, M.J. (Ed. in Chief). (1952). Great Books of the Western World: Gibbon II. (Vol. 41). Chicago, IL: Encyclopedia Britannica, Inc.

Adler, M.J. (Ed. in Chief). (1952). Great Books of the Western World: Kant. (Vol. 42). Chicago, IL: Encyclopedia Britannica, Inc.

Adler, M.J. (Ed. in Chief). (1952). Great Books of the Western World: American State Papers, The Federalist, & J.S. Mill. (Vol. 43). Chicago, IL: Encyclopedia Britannica, Inc.

Adler, M.J. (Ed. in Chief). (1952). Great Books of the Western World: Boswell. (Vol. 44). Chicago, IL: Encyclopedia Britannica, Inc.

Adler, M.J. (Ed. in Chief). (1952). Great Books of the Western World: Lavoisier, Fourier, & Faraday. (Vol. 45). Chicago, IL: Encyclopedia Britannica, Inc.
Adler, M.J. (Ed. in Chief). (1952). Great Books of the Western World: Hegel. (Vol. 46). Chicago, IL: Encyclopedia Britannica, Inc.
Adler, M.J. (Ed. in Chief). (1952). Great Books of the Western World: Goethe. (Vol. 47). Chicago, IL: Encyclopedia Britannica, Inc.
Adler, M.J. (Ed. in Chief). (1952). Great Books of the Western World: Melville. (Vol. 48). Chicago, IL: Encyclopedia Britannica, Inc.
Adler, M.J. (Ed. in Chief). (1952). Great Books of the Western World: Darwin. (Vol. 49). Chicago, IL: Encyclopedia Britannica, Inc.
Adler, M.J. (Ed. in Chief). (1952). Great Books of the Western World: Marx Engles. (Vol. 50). Chicago, IL: Encyclopedia Britannica, Inc.
Adler, M.J. (Ed. in Chief). (1952). Great Books of the Western World: Tolstoy. (Vol. 51). Chicago, IL: Encyclopedia Britannica, Inc.
Adler, M.J. (Ed. in Chief). (1952). Great Books of the Western World: Dostoevsky. (Vol. 52). Chicago, IL: Encyclopedia Britannica, Inc.
Adler, M.J. (Ed. in Chief). (1952). Great Books of the Western World: William James. (Vol. 53). Chicago, IL: Encyclopedia Britannica, Inc.
Adler, M.J. (Ed. in Chief). (1952). Great Books of the Western World: Freud. (Vol. 54). Chicago, IL: Encyclopedia Britannica, Inc.
Adler, R., Rosenfeld, L., Towne, N., & Proctor, R. (1998). Interplay: The Process of Interpersonal Communication (7th ed.). Fort Worth, TX: Harcourt Brace College Publishers. ISBN: 0-15-5039776.
Aesop. (1994). Aesop's Fables. New York: Dover Publications, Inc. ISBN: 0-486-28020-9.
Africa, T. (1991). The Immense Majesty: A History of Rome and the Roman Empire. Arlington Heights, IL: Harlan Davidson, Inc. ISBN: 0-88295-874-7.
Agee, P. (1975). Inside the Company CIA Diary. New York: Bantam Books.
Agnew, J., & Knapp, R, (1983). Linear Algebra with Applications (2nd ed.). Monterey, CA: Brooks/Cole Publishing Company. ISBN: 0-534-01364-3.
Aguayo, R. with foreword by Deming, E. (1990). Dr. Deming: The American Who Taught The Japanese About Quality. New York: Fireside, A Division of Simon & Schuster. ISBN: 0-671-74621-9.
Aismov, I. (1989). Nemesis. New York: Doubleday. ISBN: 0-7924-2661-4.
Alcott, L. (1901). Little Men: Life at Plumfield with Jo's Boys. New York: A.L. Burt Company.
Alcott, L. (1940). Little Men. Racine, WI: Whitman Publishing Company.
Alexie, S. (1993). The Lone Ranger and Tonto Fist Fight in Heaven. New York: HarperPerennial. ISBN: 0-06-097624-1.

Alighieri, D., translated by Mandelbaum, A., with and introduction by Montale, E., and notes by Armour, P. (1995). The Divine Comedy. New York: Alfred A. Knopf, Inc. ISBN: 0-679-43313-9.
Allen, C.W. (1997). Autobiography of Red Cloud: War Leader of the Oglalas. Eds. R. Eli Paul. Chelsea, MI: Montana Historical Society Press. ISBN: 0-917298-50-0.
Allen, F. (1994). Secret Formula. New York: HarperCollins. ISBN: 0-88730-672-1.
Allen, G., & Abraham, L. (1971). None Dare Call it Conspiracy. Rossmoor, CA: Concord Press.
Alzado. L., with Zimmerman, P. (1978). Mile High: The Story of Lyle Alzado and the Amazing Denver Broncos. New York: Berkley Medallion Books. ISBN: 425-03920-X.
Ambraziejus, A. (1992). Managing Time. Stamford, CT: Longmeadow Press. ISBN: 0-681-41404-9.
America Online. (1998). America Online, Inc. 1998 Annual Report: On a Mission. Dulles, VA: America Online, Inc.
American Bible Society. (Ed.). (1991). 5 Minutes a Day…Finished in a Year: Year of the Bible: New Testament. New York: American Bible Society.
American Psychiatric Association. (1994). Diagnostic and Statistical manual of Mental Disorders: DSM-IV (4th ed.). Washington, D.C.: American Psychiatric Association. ISBN: 0-89042-061-0.
American Psychological Association. (2001). Publication Manual of the American Psychological Association (5th ed.). Washington, D.C: American Psychological Association. ISBN: 1-55798-810-2.
American Studies, Vol. 41(#1). ISSN: 0026-3079.
Anderson, B. (1983). Imagined Communities: Reflections on the Origin and Spread of Nationalism. New York, NY: Verso Press. ISBN: 0-86091-546-8.
Anderson, L. (Speaker) (1990). Dear Dad: Letters from an Adult Child. (Cassette Recording). New York: Harper Audio. ISBN: 1-55994-205-3.
Andrew, C., & Mitrokhin, V. (1999). The Sword and the Shield: The Mitrokhin Archive and the Secret History of the KGB. New York, NY: Basic Books Group. ISBN: 0-465-00310-9.
Angell, N. (1929). The Story of Money. Garden City, NY: Garden City Publishing Company, Inc.
Anthony, R., & Reece, J. (1989). Accounting: Text and Cases (8th ed.). Homewood, IL: Irwin. ISBN: 0-256-03570-9.
Anzaldua, G. (1987). Borderlands. San Francisco, CA: Aunt Lute Books. ISBN: 1-879960-56-7.

Aristotle. (1981). The Politics. Eds. Betty Radice. London, England: Penguin Books. ISBN: 0-14-044421-1.
Aristotle. (1996). The Nicomachean Ethics. Ware, Hertfordshire: Wordsworth Classics of World Literature. ISBN: 1-85326-461-X.
Arkin, H., & Colton, R. (1950). Tables For Statisticians. New York: Barnes & Noble, Inc. Library of Congress Catalog Card Number: 50-3378.
Arnold, G. (1986). Computer Science Laboratory Manual (3rd ed.). Laramie, WY: University of Wyoming.
Asimov, I. (1985). Robots and Empire. New York, NY: Ballantine Books. ISBN: 0-345-3894-9.
Asimov, I. (1986). Foundation and Earth. Garden City, NY: Doubleday & Company.
Asimov, I. (1990). Robots and Aliens: Book 3; Intruder. New York: Byron Preiss Visual Publications, Inc. ISBN: 0-441-73129-5.
Askeland, D. (1984). The Science and Engineering of Materials. Monterey, CA: Brooks/Cole Engineering Division. ISBN: 0-534-02957-4.
Athearn, Robert G. (1971). Union Pacific Country. Lincoln, NE: University of Nebraska Press; A Bison Book. ISBN: 0-8032-5829-1.
Atwood, M. (1985). The Handmaid's Tale. New York: Faucett Crest. ISBN: 0-449-21260-2.
Axelrod, R. (1984). The Evolution of Cooperation. U.S.A.: Basic Books. ISBN: 0-465-02121-2.
Bacon-Smith, C. (1992). Enterprising Women: Television Fandom and the Creation of Popular Myth. Philadelphia: University of Pennsylvania Press.
Baigent, M., & Leigh, R. (1991). The Dead Sea Scrolls Deception. New York: Touchstone. ISBN: 0-671-79797-2.
Balch, W.R. (1883). The People's Universal Hand-Book and Every-Day Encyclopedia. Philadelphia, PA: Thayer, Merriam & Co.
Baldridge, L. (1989). George Washington's Rules of Civility & Decent Behavior in Company and Conversation. Mount Vernon, VI: The Mount Vernon Ladies' Association. ISBN: 0-931917-18-2.
Bales, K. (1999). Disposable People: New Slavery in the Global Economy. Berkeley and Los Angeles, CA: University of California Press. ISBN: 0-520-21797-7.
Bamford, J. (1982). The Puzzle Palace: A Report on NSA, America's Most Secret Agency. Boston, MA: Houghton Mifflin Company. ISBN: 0-395-31286-8.
Bannock, G., Baxter, R.E., & Davis, E. (1998). Dictionary of Economics. New York: John Wiley & Sons, Inc. ISBN: 0-471-29599-X.
Barber, B. (1995). Jihad vs. McWorld: How Globalism and Tribalism are Reshaping the World. New York: Ballantine Books. ISBN: 345-38304-4.

Barden, W. (1986). Electronics Data Handbook. Fort Worth, TX: Radio Shack; a division of Tandy Corporation.

Barnes, R. (1958). Motion and Time Study (4th ed.). New York: John Wiley & Sons, Inc. Library of Congress Catalog Card Number: 57-13437.

Barnet, S., Berman, M., & Burto, W. (1981). An Introduction to Literature (7th ed.). Boston, MA: Little, Brown and Company. ISBN: 0-316-082112.

Barnett, R. (1980). Analytic Trigonometry with applications (2nd ed.). Belmont, CA: Wadsworth Publishing Company. ISBN: 0-534-00728-7.

Barnett, R., & Ziegler, M. (1996). Calculus: For Business, Economics, Life Sciences, and Social Sciences (7th ed.). Upper Saddle River, NJ: Prentice Hall. ISBN: 0-13-372012-8.

Baron, R. (1995). Psychology (3rd ed.). Boston, MA: Allyn and Bacon. ISBN: 0-205-16051-4.

Barro, R. (1993). Macroeconomics (4th ed.). New York: John Wiley & Sons. ISBN: 0471-57543-7.

Barro, R. (1996). Getting it Right: Markets and Choices in a Free Society. Cambridge, MA: Massachusetts Institute of Technology Press. ISBN: 0-262-52226-8.

Bartlett, C., & Ghoshal, S. (1992). Transnational Management: Text, Cases, and Readings in Cross-Border Management. Burr Ridge, IL: Irwin. ISBN: 0-256-08485-8.

Barton, B. (Ed.). (1984). Buffalo Bones IV: Stories from Wyoming's Past. Wyoming: Wyoming State Press. ISBN: 0943398-08-8.

Batra, R. (1987). The Great Depression of 1990. New York, NY: Simon & Schuster. ISBN: 0-671-64022-4.

Baumol, W., & Blinder, A. (1991). Microeconomics: Principles and Policy (5th ed.). San Diego, CA: Harcourt Brace Jovanovich, Publishers. ISBN: 0-15-518865-8.

Baumol, W., & Blinder, A. (1994). Macroeconomics: Principles and Policy (7th ed.). Ft. Worth, TX: The Dryden Press. ISBN: 0-03-011263-X.

Baumol, W., & Blinder, A. (1994). Macroeconomics: Principles and Policy (7th ed., 1998 Update). Ft. Worth, TX: The Dryden Press. ISBN: 0-03-025051-X.

Baxter, G., & Simon, J. (1970). Wyoming Fishes (Rev. ed.). Cheyenne, WY: Wyoming Game and Fish Department.

Baye, M. (2000). Managerial Economics & Business Strategy (3rd ed.). New York: McGraw-Hill Higher Education. ISBN: 0-07-228917-1.

Bazley, J., Nikolai, L., & Grove, H. (1991). Financial Accounting: Concepts and Uses (2nd ed.). Boston, MA: PWS-Kent Publishing Company. ISBN: 0-534-92366-6.

Bear, J., & Bear, M. (1995). College Degrees by Mail (Rev. ed.). Berkeley, CA: Ten Speed Press.

Beer, F., & Johnston, E.R. (1977). Vector Mechanics for Engineers: Statics (3rd ed.). New York: McGraw-Hill Book Company. ISBN: 0-07-004278-0.

Beer, F., & Johnston, R. Jr. (1977). Vector Mechanics for Engineers: Dynamics (3rd ed.). New York: McGraw-Hill Book Company. ISBN: 0-07-004281-0.

Bell, A., & Smith, D. (1991). Winning With Difficult People. New York: Barron's Educational Series, Inc. ISBN: 0-8120-4583-1.

Belsey, C. (1992). Critical Practice. New York: Routledge.

Bentham, J. (1988). The Principles of Morals and Legislation. Amherst, New York: Prometheus Books.

Bercovitch, S., & Jehlen, M. (Ed.). (1986). Ideology and Classic American Literature: Myth and the Production of History. New York: Cambridge University Press.

Berne, E., (1964). Games People Play. New York: Grove Press. Library of Congress Catalog Card Number: 64-13783.

Berra, Y. (1998). The Yogi Book: I Really Didn't Say Everything I Said! New York, NY: Workman Publishing. ISBN: 0-7611-1090-9.

Berry, H. (1990). What They Believe: Masons. Lincoln, NE: Back To The Bible. ISBN: 0-8474-0828-0.

Besant, L. (Ed.). (1985). Commodity Training Manual. U.S.A.: Chicago Board of Trade.

Beyer, T. (1993). Barron's Russian at a Glance: Phrase Book & Dictionary for Travelers. New York: Barron's Educational Series, Inc. ISBN: 0-8120-4299-9.

Beyer, W.H. (1984). CRC Standard Mathematical Tables (27th ed.). Boca Raton, FL: CRC Press, Inc. ISBN: 0-8493-0627-2.

Binger, B., & Hoffman, E. (1998). Microeconomics with Calculus (2nd ed.). Reading, MA: Addison-Wesley Educational Publishers, Inc. ISBN: 0-321-01225-9.

Bingham, R., & Walstad, W. (1990). Study Guide to accompany McConnell and Brue: Microeconomics. New York: McGraw-Hill Publishing Company. ISBN: 0-07-045524-4.

Bissinger, H. (1990). Friday Night Lights: A Town, a Team, and a Dream. Reading, MA: Addison-Wesley Publishing Company, Inc.

Black, B. (1986). Coyote Cowboy Poetry. Wheatridge, CO: Coyote Cowboy Company. ISBN: 0-939343-00-2.

Blanchard, K., & Johnson, S. (1984). The One-Minute Manager: The Quickest Way to Increase Your Own Prosperity. New York, NY: A Berkley Book. ISBN: 0-425-06265-1.

Bodin, M. (1991). Using the Telephone More Effectively. New York: Barron's Educational Series, Inc. ISBN: 0-8120-4672-2.

Boime, A. (1991). The Magisterial Gaze: Manifest Destiny and American Landscape Painting c. 1830-1865. Hong Kong: Smithsonian Institution Press.

Boland, L. (1992). The Principles of Economics: Some Lies My Teachers Told Me. New York: Routledge. ISBN: 0-415-13208-8.

Bond, L. (1989). Red Phoenix. New York: Warner Books. ISBN: 0-446-35968-8.

Bone, Jan. (1993). Opportunities in Cable Television Careers. Lincolnwood (Chicago), IL. VGM Career Horizons. ISBN:

Boone, L., & Kurtz, D. (1990). Contemporary Business (6th ed.). Orlando, FL: The Dryden Press. ISBN: 0-03-027559-8.

Boone, L., & Kurtz, D. (1992). Management (4th ed.). New York: McGraw-Hill, Inc. ISBN: 0-07-540964-X.

Boorstin, D. (1983). The Discoverers: A History of Man's Search to Know His World and Himself. New York: Random House. ISBN: 0-394-40229-4.

Boren, H. (1992). Roman Society (2nd ed.). Lexington, MA: D.C. Heath and Company. ISBN: 0-669-17801-2.

Boroson, W. (1989). Keys To Investing in Mutual Funds. New York: Barron's Educational Series, Inc. ISBN: 0-8120-4162-3.

Boulding, K. (1970). Economics as a Science. New York: McGraw-Hill Book Company. Library of Congress Catalog Card Number: 75-105420.

Bourdieu, Pierre. (1994). Culture/Power/History: A Reader in Contemporary Social Theory. Eds. Nicholas B. Dirks, Geoff Eley, Sherry B. Ortner. Princeton U. Press. Chapter 4, *Structures, Habitus, Power: Basis for a Theory of Symbolic Power, Doxa, Orthodoxy, and Heterodoxy.*

Bowie, G.L., Michaels, M., & Solomon, R. (1996). Twenty Questions: An Introduction to Philosophy (3rd ed.). Fort Worth, TX: Harcourt Brace College Publishers. ISBN: 0-15-5026607.

Boyce, W., & DiPrima, R. (1977). Elementary Differential Equations and Boundary Value Problems (3rd ed.). New York: John Wiley & Sons. ISBN: 0-471-09334-3.

Boyce, W., & DiPrima, R. (1992). Elementary Differential Equations and Boundary Volume Problems (5th ed.). New York: John Wiley & Sons. ISBN: 0-471-50998-1.

Bradbury, R. (1953). Fahrenheit 451...The Temperature at which Books Burn. New York, NY: Ballantine Books. ISBN: 0-345-34296-8.

Bradbury, R. (Screenplay Writer), & Huston, J. (Producer and Screenplay Writer). (1996). Moby Dick. [Motion Picture]. United States: MGM/UA Home Video. ISBN: 0-7928-3247-7.

Brick, J. (1980). Bank Management: Concepts and Issues. Richmond, VA: Robert F. Dame, Inc. ISBN: 0-936328-00-2.

Brigham, E. (1995). Fundamentals of Financial Management (7th ed.). Fort Worth, TX: The Dryden Press. ISBN: 0-03-094870-3.

Bringham, E., & Gapenski, L. (1990). Cases in Financial Management: Module A. Orlando, FL: The Dryden Press. ISBN: 0-03-033223-0.

Bringham, E., & Gapenski, L. (1993). Intermediate Financial Management (4th ed.). Orlando, FL: The Dryden Press. ISBN: 0-03-075482-8.

Bromley, H., & Apple, M. (1998). Education/Technology/Power: Educational Computing as a Social Practice. Albany, NY: State University of New York. Coe Libr. Call #: LB 1028.43.E372 1998. ISBN: 0-7914-3798-1.

Brooks, P. (1984). Reading for the Plot: Design and Intention in the Narrative. New York: A.A. Knopf.

Brooks, W., & Emmert, P. (1976). Interpersonal Communication. Dubuque, IA: Wm. C. Brown Company. ISBN: 0-697-04172-7.

Brown, D. (1970). Bury my Heart at Wounded Knee: An Indian History of the American West. New York, NY: Henry Holt and Company, Inc. ISBN: 0-8050-1730-5.

Brown, Joseph Epes. (1989). *Black Elk: The Sacred Pipe.* Berkeley, CA. The University Oklahoma Press (Audio). ISBN: 0-944993-13-3.

Brown, L.K., & Mussell, K. (1984). *Ethnic and Regional Foodways in the United States: The Performance of Group Identity.* ISBN: 0-87049-419-8.

Browne, H. (Ed.). (1970). How You Can Profit From the Coming Devaluation. New Rochelle, NY: Arlington House. ISBN: 87000-073-X.

Buchan, V. (1991). Make Presentations with Confidence. New York: Barron's Educational Series, Inc. ISBN: 0-8120-4588-2.

Buchsbaum, W. (1978). Buchsbaum's Complete Handbook of Practical Electronic Reference Data (2nd ed.). Englewood Cliffs, NJ: Prentice-Hall, Inc. ISBN: 0-13-084624-4.

Buchwald, A. (1964). And Then I Told The President. Greenwich, CT: A Fawcett Crest Book. Library of Congress Catalog Card Number: 65-13289.

Buchwald, A. (1981). Laid Back in Washington. New York: Berkley Books. ISBN: 0-425-05779-8.

Buck, R. (1976). Human Motivation and Emotion. New York: John Wiley & Sons. ISBN: 0-471-11570-3.

Burack, S. (Ed.). (1989). The Writer's Handbook. Boston, MA: The Writer, Inc. Library of Congress Catalog Card Number: 36-28596.

Burns, C. (1998). Masonic and Occult Symbols Illustrated. Mt. Carmel, PA: Sharing. ISBN: 1-891117-12-2.

Burns, K. (Executive Producer), Duncan, D., Ward, G. (Writers), Ives, S., Abramson, J., & Kantor, M. (Producers) (1996). The West: The Grandest Enterprise Under God. [Motion Picture]. United States: Insignia Films. ISBN: 1-7806-1352-X.

Burns, K. (Executive Producer), Duncan, D., Ward, G. (Writers), Ives, S., Abramson, J., & Kantor, M. (Producers) (1996). The West: One Sky Above Us. [Motion Picture]. United States: Insignia Films. ISBN: 1-7806-1352-X.

Burns, K. (Executive Producer), Duncan, D., Ward, G. (Writers), Ives, S., Abramson, J., & Kantor, M. (Producers) (1996). The West: Ghost Dance. [Motion Picture]. United States: Insignia Films. ISBN: 1-7806-1352-X.

Burns, K. (Executive Producer), Duncan, D., Ward, G. (Writers), Ives, S., Abramson, J., & Kantor, M. (Producers) (1996). The West: The Geography of Hope. [Motion Picture]. United States: Insignia Films. ISBN: 1-7806-1352-X.

Burns, K. (Executive Producer), Duncan, D., Ward, G. (Writers), Ives, S., Abramson, J., & Kantor, M. (Producers) (1996). The West: Fight No More Forever. [Motion Picture]. United States: Insignia Films. ISBN: 1-7806-1352-X.

Burns, K. (Executive Producer), Duncan, D., Ward, G. (Writers), Ives, S., Abramson, J., & Kantor, M. (Producers) (1996). The West: Death Runs Riot. [Motion Picture]. United States: Insignia Films. ISBN: 1-7806-1352-X.

Burns, K. (Executive Producer), Duncan, D., Ward, G. (Writers), Ives, S., Abramson, J., & Kantor, M. (Producers) (1996). The West: The Speck of the Future. [Motion Picture]. United States: Insignia Films. ISBN: 1-7806-1352-X.

Burns, K. (Executive Producer), Duncan, D., Ward, G. (Writers), Ives, S., Abramson, J., & Kantor, M. (Producers) (1996). The West: Empire Upon the Trails. [Motion Picture]. United States: Insignia Films. ISBN: 1-7806-1352-X.

Burns, K. (Executive Producer), Duncan, D., Ward, G. (Writers), Ives, S., Abramson, J., & Kantor, M. (Producers) (1996). The West: The People. [Motion Picture]. United States: Insignia Films. ISBN: 1-7806-1352-X.

Burns, K. (Writer/Producer), & Rockwell, C. (Producer). (1996). Thomas Jefferson. [Motion Picture]. United States: Florentine Films. ISBN: 0-7806-1678-2.

Burns, K. (Writer/Producer), Ward, G. (Writer), & Novick, L. (Producer) (1994). Baseball: The First Inning: Our Game, the 1840's–1900. [Motion Picture]. United States: Florentine Films. ISBN: 0-7806-0548-9.

Burns, K. (Writer/Producer), Ward, G. (Writer), & Novick, L. (Producer) (1994). Baseball: The Second Inning: Something Like A War, 1900-1910. [Motion Picture]. United States: Florentine Films. ISBN: 0-7806-0548-9.

Burns, K. (Writer/Producer), Ward, G. (Writer), & Novick, L. (Producer) (1994). Baseball: The Third Inning: The Faith of Fifty Million People, 1910-1920. [Motion Picture]. United States: Florentine Films. ISBN: 0-7806-0548-9.

Burns, K. (Writer/Producer), Ward, G. (Writer), & Novick, L. (Producer) (1994). Baseball: The Fourth Inning: A National Heirloom, 1920-1930. [Motion Picture]. United States: Florentine Films. ISBN: 0-7806-0548-9.

Burns, K. (Writer/Producer), Ward, G. (Writer), & Novick, L. (Producer) (1994). Baseball: The Fifth Inning: Shadow Ball, 1930-1940. [Motion Picture]. United States: Florentine Films. ISBN: 0-7806-0548-9.

Burns, K. (Writer/Producer), Ward, G. (Writer), & Novick, L. (Producer) (1994). Baseball: The Sixth Inning: The National Pastime 1940-1950. [Motion Picture]. United States: Florentine Films. ISBN: 0-7806-0548-9.

Burns, K. (Writer/Producer), Ward, G. (Writer), & Novick, L. (Producer) (1994). Baseball: The Seventh Inning: The Capital of Baseball, 1950-1960. [Motion Picture]. United States: Florentine Films. ISBN: 0-7806-0548-9.

Burns, K. (Writer/Producer), Ward, G. (Writer), & Novick, L. (Producer) (1994). Baseball: The Eighth Inning: A Whole New Ballgame, 1960-1970. [Motion Picture]. United States: Florentine Films. ISBN: 0-7806-0548-9.

Burns, K. (Writer/Producer), Ward, G. (Writer), & Novick, L. (Producer) (1994). Baseball: The Ninth Inning: Home, 1970-Present. [Motion Picture]. United States: Florentine Films. ISBN: 0-7806-0548-9.

Burns, K., Kilberg, R. (Producers), & Ward, G. (Writer). (1985). Ken Burns' America Collection: Huey Long. [Motion Picture]. United States: Turner Home Entertainment. ISBN: 0-7806-0815-1.

Burns, K., Squires, B. (Producers), Weisberger, B., & Ward, G. (Writers). (1985). America: Brooklyn Bridge. [Motion Picture]. United States: Florentine Films. ISBN: 0-7806-1379-1.

Burns, K., Squires, B. (Producers), Weisberger, B., & Ward, G. (Writers). (1985). America: Empire of the Air: The Men Who Made Radio. [Motion Picture]. United States: Florentine Films. ISBN: 0-7806-1379-1.

Burns, K., Squires, B. (Producers), Weisberger, B., & Ward, G. (Writers). (1985). America: Thomas Hart Benton. [Motion Picture]. United States: Florentine Films. ISBN: 0-7806-1379-1.

Burns, K., Squires, B. (Producers), Weisberger, B., & Ward, G. (Writers). (1985). America: Huey Long. [Motion Picture]. United States: Florentine Films. ISBN: 0-7806-1379-1.

Burns, K., Squires, B. (Producers), Weisberger, B., & Ward, G. (Writers). (1985). America: The Congress. [Motion Picture]. United States: Florentine Films. ISBN: 0-7806-1379-1.

Burns, K., Squires, B. (Producers), Weisberger, B., & Ward, G. (Writers). (1985). America: The Shakers. [Motion Picture]. United States: Florentine Films. ISBN: 0-7806-1379-1.

Burns, K., Squires, B. (Producers), Weisberger, B., & Ward, G. (Writers). (1985). America: Statue of Liberty. [Motion Picture]. United States: Florentine Films. ISBN: 0-7806-1379-1.

Burrows, W. (1986). *Deep Black:* The Startling Truth Behind America's Top-Secret Spy Satellites. New York, NY: Berkley Books. ISBN: 0-425-10879-1.

Burton, C. (1998). Burton's Legal Thesaurus (3rd ed.). New York: MacMillan Library Reference USA.

Bush, G., & Gold, V. (1987). Looking Forward: An Autobiography. New York: Bantam Books. ISBN: 0-553-27791-X.

Callicott, J. Baird. (1998). *The Great New Wilderness Debate: An Expansive Collection of Writings Defining Wilderness from John Muir to Gary Snyder.* ISBN: 0-8203-1984-8.

Campbell, J., & Moyers, B. (1988). The Power of Myth. New York: Doubleday. ISBN: 0-385-24774-5.

Cannon, L. (1991). President Reagan: The Role of A Lifetime. New York: A Touchstone Book. ISBN: 0-671-75576-5.

Cardozo, B.N. (1973). The Nature of the Judicial Process. London, England: Yale University Press. ISBN: 0-300-00033-2.

Carey, G. (1970). Cliffs Notes on Sinclair's The Jungle. Lincoln, NE: Cliff's Notes, Inc. ISBN: 0-8220-0699-5.

Carnegie, D. (1981). Dale Carnegie's Lifetime Plan for Success: How to Win Friends & Influence People, How to Stop Worrying & Start Living. New York: Galahad Books. ISBN: 1-57866-039-4.

Carson, R. (1962). Silent Spring. New York, NY: Houghton Mifflin Company. ISBN: 0-395-45390-9.

Carson, R., Butcher, J., & Coleman, J. (1988). Abnormal Psychology and Modern Life (8th ed.). Glenview, IL: Scott, Foresman and Company. ISBN: 0-673-18932-5.

Cawley, G., & Horan, M. (1996). The Equality State: Government and Politics in Wyoming. Eds. Larry Hubbell. Dubuque, IA: Eddie Bowers Publishing, Inc. ISBN: 0-945483-61-9.

Chang, D. (1988). China under Deng Xiaoping: Political and Economic Reform. London, England: MacMillan Press. ISBN: 0-333-45129-5.

Chatman, S. (1978). Story and Discourse: Narrative Structure in Fiction and Film. Ithaca, NY: Cornell University Press.

Chavel, C.B. (1967). The Commandments: Volume one: The Positive Commandments. New York: The Soncino Press.

Chavel, C.B. (1967). <u>The Commandments: Volume two: The Negative Commandments.</u> New York: The Soncino Press.
Cheng, D. (1983). <u>Field and Wave Electromagnetics.</u> Reading, MA: Addison-Wesley Publishing Company. ISBN: 0-201-01239-1.
Chesterman, C. (1978). <u>The Audubon Society Field Guide To North American Rocks and Minerals.</u> New York: Alfred A. Knoph, Publisher. ISBN: 0-394-50269-8.
Chiang, A. (1984). <u>Fundamental Methods of Mathematical Economics</u> (3rd ed.). New York: McGraw-Hill, Inc. ISBN: 0-07-010813-7.
Chicago Mercantile Exchange. (Unknown). <u>The Currency Opportunity.</u> [Motion Picture]. United States: Chicago Mercantile Exchange.
Chomsky, N., with foreword by Said, E. (1999). <u>Fateful Triangle.</u> Cambridge, MA: South End Press. ISBN: 0-89608-601-1.
Chunovic, L. (Ed.). (1993). <u>Chris-In-The-Morning; Love, Life, and the Whole Karmic Enchilada.</u> Chicago, IL: Contemporary Books. ISBN: 0-8092-3762-8.
Churchill, W. (1956). <u>A History of the English Speaking Peoples: The Age of Revolution.</u> New York: Barnes & Noble Books. ISBN:0-88029-425-6.
Churchill, W. (1956). <u>A History of the English Speaking Peoples: The Birth of Britain.</u> New York, NY: Barnes and Noble Books. ISBN: 0-88029-426-4.
Churchill, W. (1958). <u>A History of the English Speaking Peoples: The Great Democracies.</u> New York: Barnes & Noble Books. ISBN: 0-88029-426-4.
Clancy, T. (1984). <u>The Hunt for Red October.</u> New York: The Berkley Publishing Group. ISBN: 0-425-12027-9.
Clancy, T. (1986). <u>Red Storm Rising.</u> New York, NY: Berkley Books. ISBN: 0-425-10107-X.
Clancy, T. (1991). <u>The Sum of All Fears.</u> New York. NY: G.P. Putnam's Sons. ISBN: 0-399-13615-0.
Clancy, T. and Horner, C. General (Ret.). (1999). *Every Man a Tiger*. New York, NY: G. P. Putnam's Sons. ISBN: 0-399-14493-5.
Clark, F., & Rimanoczy, R. (1944). <u>How We Live.</u> New York: The American Economic Foundation. Library of Congress Catalog Card Number: 60-12863.
Clark, R. (1971). <u>Einstein: The Life and Times.</u> New York: Avon. ISBN: 0-380-01159-X.
Clarke, A. (1987). <u>2061: Odyssey Three.</u> New York: Dell Rey Book. ISBN: 0-345-35173-8.
Clarkson, K., Miller, R., Jentz, G., & Cross, F. (1992). <u>West's Business Law</u> (5th ed.). St. Paul, MN: West Publishing Company. ISBN: 0-314-88944-2.
Clarkson, R. (Ed.). (1998). <u>World Champion Broncos.</u> Kansas City: Andrews McMeel Publishing. ISBN: 08362-6984-5

Coben, S., & Hill, F. (Eds.). (1966). American Economic History: Essays in Interpretation. Philadelphia, PA: J.B. Lippincott Company. Library of Congress Catalog Card Number: 66-16423.
Coggins, G. (1993). Federal Public Land and Resources Law (3rd ed.). Westbury, New York: The Foundation Press, In.ISBN: 1-56662-011-2.
Cohen, G., & Kirban, S. (1971). Revelation Visualized. Chicago, IL: Moody Press. ISBN: 0-8024-7311-3.
Cohen, W. (1991). The Practice of Marketing Management: Analysis, Planning, and Implementation (2nd ed.). New York: MacMillan Publishing Company. ISBN: 0-02-323171-8.
Colander, D.C. (1998). Microeconomics (3rd ed.). Boston, MA: Irwin McGraw-Hill. ISBN: 0-256-17273-0.
Coleman, J. (1964). Abnormal Psychology and Modern Life (3rd ed.). Atlanta, GA: Scott, Foresman and Company. Library of Congress Catalog Card Number: 64-20449.
Collins, F. (1944). How to Understand Electricity (Rev. ed.). Philadelphia, PA: The Blakiston Company.
Colodny, L., & Gettlin, R. (1991). Silent Coup: The Removal of a President. New York: St. Martin's Paperbacks. ISBN: 0-312-92763-0.
Combs, B. (1986). Westward to Promontory: Building the Union Pacific across the Plains and Mountains. New York: Crown Publishers. ISBN: 0-517-56223-5.
Consumer Reports. (1989). Consumer Reports: 1990 Buying Guide Issue. Vol. 54(#12). Mount Vernon, NY: Consumers Union of the United States, Inc. ISSN: 0010-7174.
Consumer Reports. (1990). Consumer Reports: 1991 Buying Guide Issue. Vol. 55(#12). Mount Vernon, NY: Consumers Union of the United States, Inc. ISSN: 0010-7174.
Conway, R., & Gries, D. (1979). An Introduction to Programming (3rd ed.). Boston, MA: Little, Brown and Company. ISBN: 0-316-15414-8.
Coon, D. (1992). Introduction to Psychology: Exploration and Application. St. Paul, MN: West Publishing Company. ISBN: 0-314-92211-3.
Cooper, J. (1979). The Last of The Mohicans. Norwalk, CT: The Easton Press.
Cooper, L. (2001). A Comparison of Online and Traditional Computer Applications Classes. T.H.E. Journal, Technological Horizons in Education. March 2001. (Hardcopy and see also www.thejournal.com).
Corbett, J. & Herschkowitz, M. (1935). Modern Economics. New York: The Macmillan Company.
Corley, R., Reed, O.L., & Shedd, P. (1993). The Legal and Regulatory Environment of Business (9th ed.). New York: McGraw-Hill, Inc. ISBN: 0-07-013306-9.

Cosell, H. (Speaker) (1986). I Never Played the Game (Limited ed.). (Cassette Recording). Studio City, CA: Dove Books on Tape, Inc. ISBN: 1-55800-076-3.
Cosell, H. (Speaker) (1991). What's Wrong with Sports. (Cassette Recording). New York: Simon & Schuster. ISBN: 0-671-73840-2.
Cosell, H. with Bonventre, P. (1985). I Never Played the Game. New York, NY: William Morrow and Company. ISBN: 0-380-70159-6.
Cosell, H., & Whitfield, S. (1991). What's Wrong with Sports. New York, NY: Simon & Schuster. ISBN: 0-671-70840-6.
Costner, K., Blake, M., & Wilson, J. (1990). Dances with Wolves: The Illustrated Story of the Epic Film. New York: New Market Press. ISBN: 1-55704-088-5.
Cournot, A., translated and with an introduction by Moore, M. (1956). An Essay on the Foundation of our Knowledge. New York: The Liberal Arts Press.
Cowan, R.S. (1997). A Social History of American Technology. New York, NY: Oxford University Press.
Cozzens, J.G. (1942). The Just and the Unjust. New York, NY: Harcourt, Brace & World, Inc. ISBN: 0-312-10004-3.
Cran, W. (Producer), Based on the Novel by Daniel Yergin. (1992). The Prize: The Epic Quest for Oil, Money, & Power: Programs 1 & 2, Our Plan & Empires of Oil. [Motion Picture]. United States: Public Media. ISBN: 0-7800-1271-2.
Cran, W. (Producer), Based on the Novel by Daniel Yergin. (1992). The Prize: The Epic Quest for Oil, Money, & Power: Programs 3 & 4, The Black Giant & War and Oil. [Motion Picture]. United States: Public Media. ISBN: 0-7800-1271-2.
Cran, W. (Producer), Based on the Novel by Daniel Yergin. (1992). The Prize: The Epic Quest for Oil, Money, & Power: Programs 5 & 6, Crude Diplomacy & Power to the Producers. [Motion Picture]. United States: Public Media. ISBN: 0-7800-1271-2.
Cran, W. (Producer), Based on the Novel by Daniel Yergin. (1992). The Prize: The Epic Quest for Oil, Money, & Power: Programs 7 & 8, The Tinderbox & The New Order of Oil. [Motion Picture]. United States: Public Media. ISBN: 0-7800-1271-2.
Crayton, G. (unknown). Rip Van Winkle. Philadelphia, PA: David McKay, Publisher.
Crocetti, G. (1985). GRE: Graduate Record Examination General (Aptitude) Test. New York: Arco Publishing, Inc. ISBN: 0-668-05479-4.
Cronon, W. (1996). Uncommon Ground: Rethinking the Human Place in Nature. New York, NY: W.W. Norton & Company. ISBN: 0-393-31511-8.

Crumbley, D.L., & Smith, M. (1991). Keys To Personal Financial Planning. New York: Barron's Educational Series, Inc. ISBN: 0-8120-4537-8.
Cuomo, M. (1993). More Than Words: The Speeches of Mario Cuomo. New York: St. Martin's Press.
Curchill, W. (1956). A History of the English-Speaking Peoples: The New World. New York: Barnes & Noble Books. ISBN: 0-88029-424-8.
Curtis, H. (1983). Biology (4th ed.). New York: Worth Publishers, Inc. ISBN: 0-87901-186-6.
Curwood, J. (1917). Baree, Son of Kazan. New York: Grosset & Dunlap.
Dale, N., & Orshalick, D. (1983). Introduction To PASCAL and Structured Design. Lexington, MA: D.C. Heath and Company. ISBN: 0-669-06962-0.
Dalton, J.M. (1988). How the Stock Market Works. New York, NY: New York Institute of Finance. ISBN: 0-13-435082-0.
Damore, L. (1988). Senatorial Privilege. U.S.A.: Black Star Publishing Co.
Darcy, P. (1993). Introduction to Accounting. Greenwood Village, CO: Bridge Publishing Company. ISBN: 1-881976-02-5.
Darwin, C. (1998). The Origin of Species: By Means of Natural Selection or The Preservation of Favored Races in the Struggle for Life. New York: The Modern Library. ISBN: 0-375-75146-7.
D'Augustine, C., Brown, F., Heddens, J. & Howard, C. (1970). New Dimensions in Mathematics. New York: Harper & Row. Library of Congress Catalog Card Number: 75-90252.
Davis, M. (1970). Game Theory. Toronto, Ontario, Canada: General Publishing Co. ISBN: 0-486-29672-5.
Davis, W., Pohanka, B., & Troiani, D. (Eds.). (1997). Civil War Journal: The Leaders. Nashville, TN: Rutledge Hill Press. ISBN: 1-55853-437-7.
Davis, W., Pohanka, B., & Troiani, D. (Eds.). (1998). Civil War Journal: The Battles. Nashville, TN: Rutledge Hill Press. ISBN: 1-55853-438-5.
Davis, W., Pohanka, B., & Troiani, D. (Eds.). (1999). Civil War Journal: The Legacies. Nashville, TN: Rutledge Hill Press. ISBN: 1-55853-439-3.
Davison, G., & Neale, J. (1990). Abnormal Psychology (5th ed.). New York: John Wiley & Sons. ISBN: 0-471-63108-6.
Dawood, N.J. (Translator). (1956). The Koran. New York: The Penguin Group.
Defoe, D. (1995). Robinson Crusoe. New York: Dover Publications, Inc..
Deitschmann, C. (1998). The Giants of Political Thought. New York, NY: Simon & Schuster Audio. ISBN: 0-671-57997-5.
Dell, M. with Fredman, C. (1999). Direct from Dell: Strategies That Revolutionized an Industry. New York, NY: Harper Audio. ISBN: 0-694-52023-3.

Deloria, V. Jr. (1997). <u>Red Earth; White Lies.</u> Golden, CO: Fulcrum Publishing. ISBN: 1-55591-388-1.

Deming, E. (1994). <u>The New Economics for Industry, Government, and Education</u> (2nd ed.). Cambridge, MA: Massachusetts Institute of Technology. ISBN: 0-911379-07-X.

Denholm, R., & Dolciani, M. (1971). <u>Elementary Algebra.</u> Boston, MA: Houghton Mifflin Company. ISBN: 0-395-02261-4.

Denton, J., & Schweizer, P. (Ed.). (1988). <u>Grinning with the Gipper: A Celebration of the Wit, Wisdom, and Wisecracks of Ronald Reagan.</u> New York: The Atlantic Monthly Press. ISBN: 0-87113-272-9.

Department of Defense. (March 1968). <u>In Time of Emergency: A Citizen's Handbook on Nuclear Attack and Natural Disasters.</u> Washington, D.C.: Office of Civil Defense.

Dershowitz, A. (1992). <u>Contrary to Popular Opinion.</u> New York: Pharos Books. ISBN: 0-88687-701-6.

DeVito, J. (1991). <u>Human Communication: The Basic Course</u> (5th ed.). New York: HarperCollins Publishers. ISBN: 0-06-041639-4.

Dewdney, A.K. (1988). <u>The Armchair Universe.</u> New York: W.H. Freeman & Company. ISBN: 0-716-71938-X.

Diamond, P. & Rothschild, M. (Eds.). (1989). <u>Uncertainty in Economics: Readings and Exercises</u> (Rev. ed.). San Diego, CA: Academic Press, Inc. ISBN: 0-12-214851-7.

Dickens, C. (1978). <u>The Short Stories of Charles Dickens.</u> Norwalk, CT: The Easton Press.

Dickens, C. (1981). <u>A Tale of Two Cities.</u> (Collector's Ed.). Norwalk, CT: The Easton Press.

Dixon, F. (1960). <u>#39: The Mystery of the Chinese Junk.</u> New York: Grosset & Dunlap. ISBN: 0-448-08939-4.

Dixon, F. (1962). <u>#3: The Secret of the Old Mill.</u> New York: Grosset & Dunlap. ISBN: 0-448-08903-3.

Dixon, F. (1962). <u>#41: The Clue of the Screeching Owl.</u> New York: Grosset & Dunlap. ISBN: 0-448-08941-6.

Dixon, F. (1963). <u>#42: The Viking Symbol Mystery.</u> New York: Grosset & Dunlap. ISBN: 0-448-08942-4.

Dixon, F. (1964). <u>#19: The Disappearing Floor.</u> New York: Grosset & Dunlap. ISBN: 0-448-08919-X.

Dixon, F. (1964). <u>#43: The Mystery of the Aztec Warrior.</u> New York: Grosset & Dunlap. ISBN: 0-448-08943-2.

Dixon, F. (1964). <u>#6: The Hardy Boys: The Shore Road Mystery.</u> New York: Grosset & Dunlap. ISBN: 0-448-08906-8.

Dixon, F. (1964). #7: The Secret of the Caves. New York: Grosset & Dunlap. ISBN: 0-448-08907-6.

Dixon, F. (1965). #12: Footprints Under the Window. New York: Grosset & Dunlap. ISBN: 0-448-08912-2.

Dixon, F. (1965). #16: A Figure in Hiding. New York: Grosset & Dunlap. ISBN: 0-448-08916-5.

Dixon, F. (1965). #44: The Haunted Fort. New York: Grosset & Dunlap. ISBN: 0-448-08944-0.

Dixon, F. (1965). #9: The Great Airport Mystery. New York: Grosset & Dunlap. ISBN: 0-448-08909-2.

Dixon, F. (1966). #17: The Secret Warning. New York: Grosset & Dunlap. ISBN: 0-448-08917-3.

Dixon, F. (1966). #17: The Secret Warning. New York: Grosset & Dunlap. ISBN: 0-448-08917-3.

Dixon, F. (1966). #37: The Ghost at Skeleton Rock. New York: Grosset & Dunlap. ISBN: 0-448-08937-8.

Dixon, F. (1966). #45: The Mystery of the Spiral Bridge. New York: Grosset & Dunlap. ISBN: 0-448-08945-9.

Dixon, F. (1966). #8: The Mystery of Cabin Island. New York: Grosset & Dunlap. ISBN: 0-448-08908-4.

Dixon, F. (1967). #10: What Happened at Midnight. New York: Grosset & Dunlap. ISBN: 0-448-08910-6.

Dixon, F. (1967). #13: The Mark on the Door. New York: Grosset & Dunlap. ISBN: 0-448-08913-0.

Dixon, F. (1967). #46: The Secret Agent on Flight 101. New York: Grosset & Dunlap. ISBN: 0-448-08946-7.

Dixon, F. (1968). #15: The Sinister Signpost. New York: Grosset & Dunlap. ISBN: 0-448-08915-7.

Dixon, F. (1968). #47: Mystery of the Whale Tattoo. New York: Grosset & Dunlap. ISBN: 0-448-08947-5.

Dixon, F. (1969). #31: The Secret of Wildcat Swamp. New York: Grosset & Dunlap. ISBN: 0-448-08931-9.

Dixon, F. (1969). #32: The Crisscross Shadow. New York: Grosset & Dunlap. ISBN: 0-448-08932-7.

Dixon, F. (1969). #48: The Arctic Patrol Mystery. New York: Grosset & Dunlap. ISBN: 0-448-08948-3.

Dixon, F. (1970). #23: The Melted Coins. New York: Grosset & Dunlap. ISBN: 0-448-08923-8.

Dixon, F. (1970). #49: The Bombay Boomerang. New York: Grosset & Dunlap. ISBN: 0-448-08949-1.

Dixon, F. (1971). #22: The Flickering Torch Mystery. New York: Grosset & Dunlap. ISBN: 0-448-08922-X.
Dixon, F. (1971). #33: The Yellow Feather Mystery. New York: Grosset & Dunlap. ISBN: 0-448-08933-5.
Dixon, F. (1971). #34: The Hooded Hawk Mystery. New York: Grosset & Dunlap. ISBN: 0-448-08934-3.
Dixon, F. (1971). #50: Danger on Vampire Trail. New York: Grosset & Dunlap. ISBN: 0-448-08950-5.
Dixon, F. (1972). #24: The Short-Wave Mystery. New York: Grosset & Dunlap. ISBN: 0-448-08924-6.
Dixon, F. (1972). #35: The Clue in the Embers. New York: Grosset & Dunlap. ISBN: 0-448-08935-1.
Dixon, F. (1972). #36: The Secret of Pirates' Hill. New York: Grosset & Dunlap. ISBN: 0-448-08936-X.
Dixon, F. (1972). #51: The Masked Monkey. New York: Grosset & Dunlap. ISBN: 0-448-08951-3.
Dixon, F. (1973). #38: Mystery at Devil's Paw. New York: Grosset & Dunlap. ISBN: 0-448-08938-6.
Dixon, F. (1973). #52: The Shattered Helmet. New York: Grosset & Dunlap. ISBN: 0-448-08952-1.
Dixon, F. (1974). #25: The Secret Panel. New York: Grosset & Dunlap. ISBN: 0-448-08925-4.
Dixon, F. (1974). #26: The Phantom Freighter. New York: Grosset & Dunlap. ISBN: 0-448-08926-2.
Dixon, F. (1974). #53: The Clue of the Hissing Serpent. New York: Grosset & Dunlap. ISBN: 0-448-08953-X.
Dixon, F. (1975). #27: The Secret of Skull Mountain. New York: Grosset & Dunlap. ISBN: 0-448-08927-0.
Dixon, F. (1975). #54: The Mysterious Caravan. New York: Grosset & Dunlap. ISBN: 0-448-08954-8.
Dixon, F. (1976). #28: The Sign of the Crooked Arrow. New York: Grosset & Dunlap. ISBN: 0-448-08928-9.
Dixon, F. (1976). #55: The Witchmaster's Key. New York: Grosset & Dunlap. ISBN: 0-448-08955-6.
Dixon, F. (1977). #20: Mystery of the Flying Express. New York: Grosset & Dunlap. ISBN: 0-448-08920-3.
Dixon, F. (1977). #21: The Clue of the Broken Blade. New York: Grosset & Dunlap. ISBN: 0-448-08921-1.
Dixon, F. (1977). #29: The Secret of the Lost Tunnel. New York: Grosset & Dunlap. ISBN: 0-448-08929-7.

Dixon, F. (1977). #56: The Jungle Pyramid. New York: Grosset & Dunlap. ISBN: 0-448-08956-4.

Dixon, F. (1978). #57: The Firebird Rocket. New York: Grosset & Dunlap. ISBN: 0-448-08958-2.

Dixon, F. (1979). #30: The Wailing Siren Mystery. New York: Grosset & Dunlap. ISBN: 0-448-08930-0.

Dixon, F. (1979). #48: The Sting of the Scorpion. New York: Grosset & Dunlap. ISBN: 0-448-08958-0.

Dixon, F. (1980). #61: The Hardy Boys: The Pentagon Spy. New York: A Minstrel Book. ISBN: 0-671-67221-5.

Dixon, F. (1987). #1: The Tower Treasure. New York: Grosset & Dunlap. ISBN: 0-448-08964-5.

Dixon, F. (1987). #2: The House on The Cliff. New York: Grosset & Dunlap. ISBN: 0-448-08964-5.

Dixon, F. (1987). #2: The House on The Cliff. New York: Grosset & Dunlap. ISBN: 0-448-08902-5.

Dixon, F. (1988). #92: The Hardy Boys: The Shadow Killers. New York: A Minstrel Book. ISBN: 0-671-66309-7.

Dixon, F. (1989). #40: Mystery of the Desert Giant. New York: Grosset & Dunlap. ISBN: 0-448-08940-8.

Dixon, F. (1990). #11: The Hardy Boys: While the Clock Ticked. New York: Grosset & Dunlap. ISBN: 0-448-08911-4.

Dixon, F. (1990). #14: The Hidden Harbor Mystery. New York: Grosset & Dunlap. ISBN: 0-448-08914-9.

Dixon, F. (1990). #4: The Missing Chums. New York: Grosset & Dunlap. ISBN: 0-448-08904-1.

Dixon, F. (1991). #5: Hunting for Hidden Gold. New York: Grosset & Dunlap. ISBN: 0-448-08905-X.

Doenitz, K., & translated by Stevens, R.H. (1959). Memoirs: Ten Years and Twenty Days. Cleveland, OH: The World Publishing Company. Library of Congress Catalog Card Number: 59-11530.

Dolan, E. (1983). Basic Economics (3rd ed.). Chicago, IL: The Dryden Press. ISBN: 0-03-062381-2.

Dolciani, M., Berman, S., & Freilich, J. (1965). Modern Algebra: Structure and Method. Boston, MA: Houghton Mifflin Company.

Dolciani, M., Wooton, W., Beckenbach, E., & Chinn, W. (1970). Modern School Mathematics: Structure and Method. Boston, MA: Houghton Mifflin Company.

Dolciani, M., Wooton, W., Beckenbach, E., & Markert, W. (1970). <u>Modern School Mathematics: Structure and Method.</u> Boston, MA: Houghton Mifflin Company.

Donahue, D.L. (1999). <u>The Western Range Revisited: Removing Livestock from Public Lands to Conserve Native Biodiversity.</u> Norman, OK: University of Oklahoma Press. ISBN: 0-8061-3176-4.

Donalson, S. (1987). <u>Hold On, Mr. President!</u> New York, NY: Random House. ISBN: 0-394-55393-4.

Dorf, R. (1986). <u>Modern Control Systems</u> (4th ed.). Reading, MA: Addison-Wesley Publishing Company. ISBN: 0201-05326-8.

Dorfman, R., Samuelson, P., & Solow, R. (1958). <u>Linear Programming and Economic Analysis.</u> Mineola, NY: Dover Publications, Inc. ISBN: 0-486-65491-5.

Dornbusch, R., & Fischer, S. (1990). <u>Macroeconomics</u> (5th ed.). New York: McGraw-Hill Publishing Company. ISBN: 0-07-017787-2.

Dorst, J. (1989). <u>The Written Suburb: An American Site, An Ethnographic Dilemma.</u> Philadelphia, PA: University of Pennsylvania Press. ISBN: 0-8122-1282-7.

Dorst, J. (1999). <u>Looking West.</u> Philadelphia, PA: University of Pennsylvania Press. ISBN: 0-8122-3173-2.

Dorst, J.D. (1989). <u>The Written Suburb: An American Site, An Ethnographic Dilemma.</u> Philadelphia, PA: University of Pennsylvania Press. ISBN: 0-8122-1282-7.

Dorst, J.D. (1999). <u>Looking West</u>. Philadelphia, PA: University of Pennsylvania Press. ISBN: 0-8122-1440-4.

Dougherty, C. (1992). <u>Introduction to Econometrics.</u> New York: Oxford University Press. ISBN: 0-19-504346-4.

Downes, J., & Goodman, J. (1987). <u>Dictionary of Finance and Investment Terms</u> (2nd ed.). New York: Barron's Educational Series. ISBN: 0-8120-2522-9.

Drucker, P. (1966, 1967). <u>The Effective Executive.</u> New York: HarperBusiness, A Division of HarperCollins. ISBN: 0-06-091209-X.

Drucker, P. (1981). <u>Toward the Next Economics and Other Essays</u>. New York, NY: Harper & Row Publishers, Inc. ISBN: 0-06-014828-4.

Drucker, P. (1999). <u>Management Challenges for the 21st Century.</u> New York: HarperBusiness, A Division of HarperCollins. ISBN: 0-88730-998-4.

DuBrin, A. (1992). <u>Human Relations: A Job Oriented Approach</u> (5th ed.). Englewood Cliffs, NJ: Prentice-Hall, Inc. ISBN: 0-13-395526-5.

Durant, W. (1966). <u>The Story of Civilization: The Life of Greece.</u> New York: MJF Books. ISBN: 1-56731-013-3.

Eban, A. (1984). <u>Heritage: Civilization and the Jews.</u> New York: Summit Books.

Eberly, D. (Ed.). (1994). Building a Community of Citizens: Civil Society in the 21st Century. Lanham, MD: University Press of America, Inc. ISBN: 0-8191-9614-2.

Ebert, R. (1991). Roger Ebert's Movie Home Companion (1992 ed.). Kansas City, MO: Andrews and McMeel. ISBN: 0-8362-6242-5.

Ebert, R. (1992). Roger Ebert's Movie Home Companion (1993 ed.). Kansas City, MO: Andrews and McMeel. ISBN: 0-8362-6243-3.

Ebert, R. (1993). Robert Ebert's Video Companion (1994 ed.). Kansas City, MO: Andrews and McMeel. ISBN: 0-8362-6244.

Ebert, R. (1994). Ebert's Little Movie Glossary. Kansas City, MO: Andrews and McMeel. ISBN: 0-8362-8071-7.

Ebert, R. (1994). Robert Ebert's Video Companion (1995 ed.). Kansas City, MO: Andrews and McMeel. ISBN: 0-8362-6248-4.

Ebert, R. (1995). Robert Ebert's Video Companion (1996 ed.). Kansas City, MO: Andrews and McMeel. ISBN: 0-8362-0457-3.

Ebert, R. (1996). Robert Ebert's Video Companion (1997 ed.). Kansas City, MO: Andrews and McMeel. ISBN: 0-8362-2152-4.

Ebert, R. (1997). Robert Ebert's Video Companion (1998 ed.). Kansas City, MO: Andrews and McMeel. ISBN: 0-8362-3688-2.

Ebert, R. (1998). Robert Ebert's Movie Yearbook (1999 ed.). Kansas City, MO: Andrews and McMeel. ISBN: 0-8362-6831-8.

Ebert, R. (1999). Robert Ebert's Movie Yearbook (2000 ed.). Kansas City, MO: Andrews and McMeel. ISBN: 0-7407-0027-8.

Ebert, R. (2000). Robert Ebert's Movie Yearbook (2001 ed.). Kansas City, MO: Andrews and McMeel. ISBN: 0-7407-1089-3.

Ebert, R. (2001). Rober Ebert's Movie Yearbook. Kansas City: Andrews McMeel Publishing.

Economics and Statistics Administration. (1990). Statistical Abstract of the United States (110th ed.). Washington, D.C.: U.S. Department of Commerce. Library of Congress Catalog Card Number: 4-18089.

Economics and Statistics Administration. (1996). Statistical Abstract of the United States (116th ed.). Washington, D.C.: U.S. Department of Commerce. ISBN: 0-16-048836-2.

Edmonds, D. (1999). The Oxford Reverse Dictionary. New York: Oxford University Press.

Ehrlichman, J. (1986). The China Card. New York: Simon & Schuster. ISBN: 0-671-50716-8.

Einstein, A., & translated by Harris, A. (1934). Essays in Science. New York: Philosophical Library, Inc.

Einstein, A., & translated by Lawson, R. (1995). Relativity. Amherst, NY: Prometheus Books. ISBN: 0-87975-979-8.

Ekins, P. (1992). A New World Order: Grassroots Movements for Global Change. New York: Routledge. ISBN: 0-415-07115-1.

Elgin, S. (1987). The Last Word on The Gentle Art of Verbal Self-Defense. New York: Prentice Hall Press.

Empiricus, S. (1994). Outlines of Scepticism. London, England: Cambridge University Press. ISBN: 0-521-31206-X.

———-Epstein, I. (Ed.) Cohen, A. (Actual Editor)(1965). The Babylonian Talmud: Minor Tractates. (Hebrew-English ed.). London: The Soncino Press. ISBN: 0-900689-86-2.

Epstein, I. (Ed.). (1977). The Babylonian Talmud: Seder Nashim: Gittin. (Hebrew-English ed.). London: The Soncino Press. ISBN: 0-871055-30-X.

Epstein, I. (Ed.). (1977). The Babylonian Talmud: Seder Nashim: Kiddushin. (Hebrew-English ed.). London: The Soncino Press. ISBN: 0-871055-40-7.

Epstein, I. (Ed.). (1977). The Babylonian Talmud: Seder Nezikin: Baba Kamma. (Hebrew-English ed.). London: The Soncino Press. ISBN: 0-871055-35-0.

Epstein, I. (Ed.). (1983). The Babylonian Talmud: 'Erubin. (Hebrew-English ed.). London: The Soncino Press. ISBN: 0-900689-41-2.

Epstein, I. (Ed.). (1983). The Babylonian Talmud: Seder Mo'ed: Pesahim. (Hebrew-English ed.). London: The Soncino Press. ISBN: 0-900689-81-1.

Epstein, I. (Ed.). (1983). The Babylonian Talmud: Seder Mo'ed: Rosh Hashanah, Bezah, & Shekalim. (Hebrew-English ed.). London: The Soncino Press. ISBN: 0-900689-82-X.

Epstein, I. (Ed.). (1984). The Babylonian Talmud: Seder Mo'ed: Sukkah. (Hebrew-English ed.). London: The Soncino Press. ISBN: 0-900689-83-8.

Epstein, I. (Ed.). (1984). The Babylonian Talmud: Seder Mo'ed: Ta'anith, Megillah, & Hagigah. (Hebrew-English ed.). London: The Soncino Press. ISBN: 0-900689-84-6.

Epstein, I. (Ed.). (1984). The Babylonian Talmud: Seder Nashim: Yebamoth. (Hebrew-English ed.). London: The Soncino Press. ISBN: 0-900689-97-8.

Epstein, I. (Ed.). (1984). The Babylonian Talmud: Seder Zera'im: Berakoth. (Hebrew-English ed.). London: The Soncino Press. ISBN: 0-900689-56-0.

Epstein, I. (Ed.). (1985). The Babylonian Talmud: Seder Nashim: Nazir & Sotah. (Hebrew-English ed.). London: The Soncino Press. ISBN: 0-900689-95-1.

Epstein, I. (Ed.). (1985). The Babylonian Talmud: Seder Nashim: Nedarim. (Hebrew-English ed.). London: The Soncino Press. ISBN: 0-900689-90-0.

Epstein, I. (Ed.). (1986). The Babylonian Talmud: Seder Nashim: Baba Mezia. (Hebrew-English ed.). London: The Soncino Press. ISBN: 0-900689-56-0.

Epstein, I. (Ed.). (1987). The Babylonian Talmud: Seder Mo'ed: Shabbath. (Hebrew-English ed.). London: The Soncino Press. ISBN: 0-900689-90-0.

Epstein, I. (Ed.). (1987). The Babylonian Talmud: Seder Nezikin: Sanhedrin. (Hebrew-English ed.). London: The Soncino Press. ISBN: 0-900689-88-9.

Epstein, I. (Ed.). (1987). The Babylonian Talmud: Seder Nezikin: Shebu'oth, & Makkoth. (Hebrew-English ed.). London: The Soncino Press. ISBN: 0-900689-96-X.

Epstein, I. (Ed.). (1988). The Babylonian Talmud: Seder Kodashim: Bekoroth & 'Arakin. (Hebrew-English ed.). London: The Soncino Press. ISBN: 0-900689-99-4.

Epstein, I. (Ed.). (1988). The Babylonian Talmud: Seder Kodashim: Zebahim. (Hebrew-English ed.). London: The Soncino Press. ISBN: 0-900689-93-5.

Epstein, I. (Ed.). (1988). The Babylonian Talmud: Seder Nezikin: Abodah Zarah, Horayoth, Eduyyoth, & Aboth. (Hebrew-English ed.). London: The Soncino Press. ISBN: 0-900689-89-7.

Epstein, I. (Ed.). (1989). The Babylonian Talmud: Mishnayoth Tohoroth: Kelim, Oholoth, Nega'im, Parah, Tohoroth, Mikwaoth, Makshirin, Zabim, Tebul Yom, Yadayim, & 'Ukzin. (Hebrew-English ed.). London: The Soncino Press. ISBN: 0-871055008.

Epstein, I. (Ed.). (1989). The Babylonian Talmud: Mishnayoth Zera'im: Peah, Demai, Kil'ayim, Shebi'ith, Terumoth, Ma'aseroth, Ma'aser Sheni, Hallah, 'Orlah, & Bikkurim. (Hebrew-English ed.). London: The Soncino Press. ISBN: 0-871055059.

Epstein, I. (Ed.). (1989). The Babylonian Talmud: Seder Kodashim: Temurah, Kerithoth, Me'ilah, Kinnim, Tamid, & Middoth. (Hebrew-English ed.). London: The Soncino Press. ISBN: 0-900689-61-7.

Epstein, I. (Ed.). (1989). The Babylonian Talmud: Seder Kodashim: Menahoth. (Hebrew-English ed.). London: The Soncino Press. ISBN: 0-900689-98-6.

Epstein, I. (Ed.). (1989). The Babylonian Talmud: Seder Kodashim: Hullin. (Hebrew-English ed.). London: The Soncino Press. ISBN: 0-900689-17-X.

Epstein, I. (Ed.). (1989). The Babylonian Talmud: Seder Mo'ed: Yoma. (Hebrew-English ed.). London: The Soncino Press. ISBN: 0-871055-25-3.

Epstein, I. (Ed.). (1989). The Babylonian Talmud: Seder Nashim: Kethuboth. (Hebrew-English ed.). London: The Soncino Press. ISBN: 0-871055-10-5.

Epstein, I. (Ed.). (1989). The Babylonian Talmud: Seder Nashim: Kethuboth. (Hebrew-English ed.). London: The Soncino Press. ISBN: 871055-10-5.

Epstein, I. (Ed.). (1989). The Babylonian Talmud: Seder Nezikin: Baba Bathra. (Hebrew-English ed.). London: The Soncino Press. ISBN: 0-900689-64-1.

Epstein, I. (Ed.). (1989). The Babylonian Talmud: Seder Tohoroth: Niddah. (Hebrew-English ed.). London: The Soncino Press. ISBN: 0-900689-94-3.

Epstein, I. (Ed.). (1990). The Babylonian Talmud: Index Volume. (Hebrew-English ed.). London: The Soncino Press. ISBN: 0-871055-55-5.

Esquivel, L. (1989). Like Water for Chocolate. New York, NY: Anchor Books. ISBN: 0-385-42017-X.

Evans, A., Mullen, J., & Smith, D. (1985). Basic Electronics Technology. Fort Worth, TX: Radio Shack; a division of Tandy Corporation.

Evans, J., & Berman, B. (1988). Principles of Marketing (2nd ed.). New York: Macmillan Publishing Company. ISBN: 0-02-334340-0.

Evans, R. (Producer), & Polanski, R. (Writer). (1998). Chinatown. [Motion Picture]. United States: Paramount. ISBN: 0-7921-4748-0.

Eyre, C. (Writer), & Baerwolf, R. & Suhr, R. (Producers). (Unknown). Smoke Signals. [Motion Picture]. United States: ShadowCatcher Entertainment. ISBN: 0-7888-1371-4.

Famighetti, R., Foley, J., & McGuire, T. (Eds.). (1993). The World Almanac. Mahwah, NJ: World Almanac: An Imprint of Funk & Wagnalls. ISBN: 0-88687-745-8.

Farley, J. (1990). Sociology. Englewood Cliffs, NJ: Prentice Hall. ISBN: 0-13-816000-7.

Farris, M., & Sampson, R. (1973). Public Utilities, Regulation, Management, and Ownership. Boston, MA: Houghton Mifflin Company. ISBN: 0-395-13884-1.

Faulkner, W. (1994). Big Woods: The Hunting Stories. New York: Vintage Books.

Federal Reserve Bank of Kansas City. (1997). Financing Rural America. U.S.A.: Federal Reserve Bank of Kansas City.

Feinstein, J. (1988). A Season Inside: One Year in College Basketball. New York: Villard Books.

Feinstein, J. (1989). A Season on the Brink: A Year with Bobby Knight and the Indiana Hoosiers. New York: A Fireside Book by Simon and Schuster Trade.

Feinstein, J. (1990). Forever's Team: The Story of the 1977-1978 Duke University Basketball Team. : Simon & Schuster Trade Paperbacks.

Feinstein, J. (1998). A March to Madness: The View from the Floor in the Atlantic Coast Conference. New York: Little, Brown & Company.

Feinstein, J. (2000). The Last Amateurs: Playing for Glory and Honor in Division I College Basketball. New York: Little Brown and Company.

Ferguson, K. (1991). Stephen Hawking: Quest for a Theory of Everything. New York: Bantam Books. ISBN: 0-553-29895-X.

Ferguson, M., & with foreword by Naisbitt, J. (1980, 1987). The Aquarian Conspiracy: Personal and Social Transformation in Our Time. Los Angeles, CA: J. P. Tarcher, Inc. ISBN: 0-87477-458-6.

Fernandez, M. (1999). Electronic Versus Paper: Do Children Learn from Stories on the Computer? *Learning & Leading With Technology.* Vol. 26. No 8. May 1999. Pp. 32-34.

Field, S. (1984). The Screenwriter's Workbook. New York: Dell Publishing. ISBN: 0-440-58225-3.

Field, S. (1989). Selling a Screenplay: The Screenwriter's Guide to Hollywood. New York: Dell Publishing. ISBN: 0-440-50244-6.

Fields. W.C. (1990). The Day I Drank A Glass of Water. (Cassette Recording). Minneapolis, MN: Metacom, Inc. ISBN: 0-88676-007-0.

Finamore, F.J. (Ed.). (1999). Half Hours with the Best Thinkers. New York, NY: Gramercy Books. ISBN: 0-517-20432-0.

Finkelstein, J., & Thimm, A. (1973). Economists and Society. New York: Harper & Row Publishers. ISBN: 06-046599-9.

Fischer, K., & Lazerson, A. (1984). Human Development: From Conception Through Adolescence. New York: W.H. Freeman and Company. ISBN: 0-7167-1575-9.

Fisher, C., Dwyer, D., & Yocam, K., (Eds.). (1996). Reflections on Computing in Classrooms. *Education and Technology.* San Francisco, CA: Apple Press. Jossey Bass Publishers. Coe Libr. Call #: LB 1028.5.E295 1996. ISBN: 0-7879-0238-1.

Fisher, R., & Ury, W. (1981). Getting to Yes: Negotiating Agreement Without Giving In. New York: Penguin Books. ISBN: 0 14 00.6534 2.

Fitch, T. (1990). Dictionary of Banking Terms. New York: Barron's Educational Series. ISBN: 0-8120-3946-7.

Flatt, J., & Fisher, P. (Eds.). (1981). The World Almanac and Book of Facts (1982 ed.). New York: Newspaper Enterprise Association, Inc. ISBN: 0-911818-22-7.

Flatt, J., & Fisher, P. (Eds.). (1984). The World Almanac and Book of Facts (1985 ed.). New York: Newspaper Enterprise Association, Inc. ISBN: 0-911818-71-5.

Foote, S. (1958). The Civil War: A Narrative: Fort Sumter to Perryville. New York: Vintage Books. ISBN: 0-394-74913-8.

Foote, S. (1963). The Civil War: A Narrative: Fredericksburg to Meridian. New York: Vintage Books. ISBN: 0-394-74913-8.

Foote, S. (1974). The Civil War: A Narrative: Red River to Appomattox. New York: Vintage Books. ISBN: 0-394-74913-8.

Foucault, M. (1977). Discipline and Punish: The Birth of the Prison. New York, NY: Pantheon Books. ISBN: 0-394-49942-5.

Fowler, H.W., & Gowers, E. (Ed.). (1965). A Dictionary of Modern English Usage (2nd ed., Rev.). New York: Oxford University Press. ISBN: 0-19-869115-7.

Fox, G. (1997). Reason and Reality in the Methodologies of Economics: An Introduction. Bodmin, Cornwall, Great Britain: Hartnolls Limited. ISBN: 1-84064-139-8.

Fox, R., & Mc Donald, A. (1985). Introduction to Fluid Mechanics (3rd ed.). New York: John Wiley & Sons. ISBN: 0-471-88598-3.

Frank, R., & Cook, P. (1995). The Winner-Take-All Society: Why the Few at the Top Get So Much More Than the Rest of Us. New York: The Penguin Group. ISBN: 0-02-874034-3.

Frank, Y. (1991). The Practical Talmud Dictionary. Jerusalem, Israel: The Ariel Institute. ISBN: 0-87306-588-3.

Fredriksen, P. (1988). From Jesus to Christ. New Haven: Yale University.

Freud, S. (1995). The Basic Writings of Sigmund Freud: Psychopathy of Everyday Life (1904); *The Interpretation of Dreams (1900); Three Contributions to the Theory of Sex (1905); Wit and Its Relations to the Unconscious (1905); Totem and Taboo (1913); The History of the Psychoanalytic Movement.* New York: The Modern Library. ISBN: 0-679-60166-X.

Friedan, B. (1974). The Feminine Mistique. New York, NY: Dell Publishing Co. ISBN: 0-440-32498-X.

Friedman, F., & Koffman, E. (1981). Problem Solving and Structured Programming in Fortran (2nd ed.). Reading, MA: Addison-Wesley Publishing Company. ISBN: 0-201-02461-6.

Friedman, M. (1962). Capitalism and Freedom: The Classic Statement of Milton Friedman's Economic Philosophy. Chicago, IL: The University of Chicago Press. ISBN: 0-226-26401-7.

Friedman, M., & Schwartz A. Jacobson (1963). A Monetary History of the United States, 1867-1960. Princeton, NJ: Princeton University Press. ISBN:0-691-00354-8.

Friedman, R.I. (2000). Red Mafia: How the Russian Mob has Invaded America. New York, NY: Little, Brown and Company. ISBN: 0-316-29474-8.

Friedman, T.L. (1989). From Beirut to Jerusalem. New York, NY: Anchor Books. ISBN: 0-385-41372-6.

Friedman, T.L. (1999). The Lexus and the Olive Tree: Understanding Globalization. New York, NY: Farrar Straus Giroux. ISBN: 0-374-19203-0.

Frisch, M. with photographs by Rogovin, M. (1993). Portraits in Steel. Ithaca, NY: Cornell University Press. ISBN: 0-8014-2253-1.

Frisch, M., & Rogovin, M. 1993). Portraits in Steel. Ithica, NY: Cornell University Press. ISBN: 0-8014-8102-3.

Fritz, R. (1987). Nobody Gets Rich Working for Somebody Else: An Entrepreneur's Guide. New York: Dodd, Mead, & Company.
Gabaccia, D. (1998). We Are What We Eat: Ethnic Food and the Making of Americans. Cambridge, MA. Harvard University Press. ISBN: 0-647-00190-7.
Galbraith, J. (1954). The Great Crash; 1929. New York: Mariner Books. ISBN: 0-395-85999-9.
Galbraith, J. (1958). The Affluent Society. Boston, MA: Houghton Mifflin Company.
Galbraith, J. (1973). Economics & The Public Purpose. Boston, MA: Houghton Mifflin Company. ISBN: 0-395-17206-3.
Galbraith, J. (1990). A Short History of Financial Euphoria. New York: The Penguin Group. ISBN: 0-670-85028-4.
Garner, A. [Editor] (1996). Black's Law Dictionary. St. Paul, MN: West Group.
Garraty, J., & Gay, P., with foreword by McGill, W. (Eds.). (1972). The Columbia History of the World. New York: Harper & Row. ISBN: 0-88029-004-8.
Gast, L. & Hackford, T. (Writers) & Sonenberg, D. (Producer). (1996). When We Were Kings. [Motion Picture]. United States: PolyGram Video.
Gastelum, F. (designer) (1995). Registered Representative Series 7 Study Program: Practice Examinations. Unknown: Edward Fleur Financial Education Corporation.
Gastelum, F. (designer) (1995). Registered Representative Series 7 Study Program: Volume 1. Unknown: Edward Fleur Financial Education Corporation.
Gastelum, F. (designer) (1995). Registered Representative Series 7 Study Program: Volume 2. Unknown: Edward Fleur Financial Education Corporation.
Gates, B. with Hemingway, C. (1999). Business @ The Speed of Thought: Using a Digital Nervous System. New York, NY: Warner Books. ISBN: 0-446-52568-5.
Gates, B., Myhrvold, N., & Rinearson, P. (1995). The Road Ahead. New York, NY: Penguin Books. ISBN: 0-14-026040-4.
Gay, G., & Kolb, R. (1982). Interest Rate Futures: Concepts and Issues. Richmond, VA: Robert F. Dame, Inc. ISBN: 0-936-328-19-3.
Geertz, C. (1973). The Interpretation of Cultures. Chapter I/Thick Description: Toward an Interpretive Theory of Culture. Basic Books.
Geertz, C. (1973). The Interpretation of Cultures. New York: Basic Books.
Geiogamah, H. (Writer), Grant, M. (Writer/Producer), & Foulkrod, P. (Producer). (1994). The Native Americans: The Nations of the Northeast. [Motion Picture]. United States: TBS Productions. ISBN: 0-7806-0589-6.

Geiogamah, H. (Writer), Grant, M. (Writer/Producer), & Foulkrod, P. (Producer). (1994). The Native Americans: The Tribal People of the Northwest. [Motion Picture]. United States: TBS Productions. ISBN: 0-7806-0589-6.

Geiogamah, H. (Writer), Grant, M. (Writer/Producer), & Foulkrod, P. (Producer). (1994). The Native Americans: The Tribes of the Southeast. [Motion Picture]. United States: TBS Productions. ISBN: 0-7806-0589-6.

Geiogamah, H. (Writer), Grant, M. (Writer/Producer), & Foulkrod, P. (Producer). (1994). The Native Americans: The Natives of the Southwest. [Motion Picture]. United States: TBS Productions. ISBN: 0-7806-0589-6.

Geiogamah, H. (Writer), Grant, M. (Writer/Producer), & Foulkrod, P. (Producer). (1994). The Native Americans: The People of the Great Plains (Part One). [Motion Picture]. United States: TBS Productions. ISBN: 0-7806-0589-6.

Geiogamah, H. (Writer), Grant, M. (Writer/Producer), & Foulkrod, P. (Producer). (1994). The Native Americans: The People of the Great Plains (Part Two). [Motion Picture]. United States: TBS Productions. ISBN: 0-7806-0589-6.

Gerstenberg, C. (1924). Materials of Corporation Finance (5th ed.). New York: Prentice-Hall, Inc.

Gibbon, E. (1980). The Decline and Fall of the Roman Empire. Eds. & Abridged. Dero A. Saunders. New York, NY: Penguin Books. ISBN: 0-14-043189-6.

Gibbons, R. (1992). Game Theory for Applied Economics. Princeton, NJ: Princeton University Press. ISBN: 0-691-04308-6.

Gieck, K. (1986). Engineering Formulas (5th ed.). New York: McGraw-Hill Book Company. ISBN: 0-07-023231-8.

Gifford, D., Gazecki, W., & McNulty, M. (Writers), & Gifford, D. & Gifford, A.S. (Producers). (1997). Waco: The Rules of Engagement. [Motion Picture]. United States: New Yorker Video. ISBN: 1-56730-173-8.

Gifford, F., & Waters, H. (1993). The Whole Ten Yards. New York: Random House. ISBN: 0-679-41543-2.

Gifford, F., with Mangel, C. (1976). Gifford on Courage. New York, NY: Bantam Books. ISBN: 0-553-10699-6.

Gifis, S. (1991). Law Dictionary. New York: Barron's.

Gilder, G. (1993). Wealth & Poverty. San Francisco, CA: ICS Press. ISBN: 1-55815-240-7.

Gilder, G. (1994). Life after Television. New York, NY: W.W. Norton & Company. ISBN: 0-393-31158-9.

Gilder, G. (2000). Telecosm: How Infinite Bandwidth will Revolutionize our World. New York: The Free Press. ISBN: 0-684-80930-3.

Gilmore, G. (1977). The Ages of American Law. Chelsea, Michigan: Yale University Press. ISBN: 0-300-02352-9.

Gingrich, N. (1998). Lessons Learned the Hard Way: A Personal Report. New York: HarperCollins. ISBN: 0-06-019106-6.

Gingrich, N. (1995). To Renew America. New York, NY: HarperCollins Publishers. ISBN: 0-06-017336-X.

Gingrich, N. (1995). Toward American Renewal. [Motion Picture]. United States: Neil Romano & Associates, Inc.

Gingrich, N. (February 11th, 1995). Renewing American Civilization, A Project of the Progress & Freedom Foundation: Tape 6: Pillar Five: Quality as Defined by Deming. [Motion Picture]. (Available from Renewing American Civilization, 816 South Chapman Street, Greensboro, NC, 27403)

Gingrich, N. (February 18, 1995). Renewing American Civilization, A Project of the Progress & Freedom Foundation: Tape 7: Third Wave and American Civilization. [Motion Picture]. (Available from Renewing American Civilization, 816 South Chapman Street, Greensboro, NC, 27403)

Gingrich, N. (February 25th, 1995). Renewing American Civilization, A Project of the Progress & Freedom Foundation: Tape 8: Creating American Jobs in the World Market. [Motion Picture]. (Available from Renewing American Civilization, 816 South Chapman Street, Greensboro, NC, 27403)

Gingrich, N. (February 4th, 1995). Renewing American Civilization, A Project of the Progress & Freedom Foundation: Tape 5: Pillar Four: The Spirit of Invention and Discovery. [Motion Picture]. (Available from: Renewing American Civilization, 816 South Chapman Street, Greensboro, NC, 27403)

Gingrich, N. (January 14th, 1995). Renewing American Civilization, A Project of the Progress & Freedom Foundation: Tape 2: Pillar One: The Historic Lessons of American Civilization. [Motion Picture]. (Available from Renewing American Civilization, 816 South Chapman Street, Greensboro, NC, 27403)

Gingrich, N. (January 21st, 1995). Renewing American Civilization, A Project of the Progress & Freedom Foundation: Tape 3: Pillar Two: Personal Strength. [Motion Picture]. (Available from Renewing American Civilization, 816 South Chapman Street, Greensboro, NC, 27403)

Gingrich, N. (January 28th, 1995). Renewing American Civilization, A Project of the Progress & Freedom Foundation: Tape 4: Pillar Three: Entrepreneurial Free Enterprise. [Motion Picture]. (Available from Renewing American Civilization, 816 South Chapman Street, Greensboro, NC, 27403)

Gingrich, N. (January 7th, 1995). Renewing American Civilization, A Project of the Progress & Freedom Foundation: Tape 1: American Civilization. [Motion Picture]. (Available from Renewing American Civilization, 816 South Chapman Street, Greensboro, NC, 27403)

Gingrich, N. (March 11th, 1995). Renewing American Civilization, A Project of the Progress & Freedom Foundation: Tape 10: Citizenship and Community in 21st Century America. [Motion Picture]. (Available from Renewing American Civilization, 816 South Chapman Street, Greensboro, NC, 27403)

Gingrich, N. (March 4th, 1995). Renewing American Civilization, A Project of the Progress & Freedom Foundation: Tape 9: Replacing the Culture of Violence and Poverty with a Culture of Productivity and Safety. [Motion Picture]. (Available from Renewing American Civilization, 816 South Chapman Street, Greensboro, NC, 27403)

Gintis, H. (2000). Game Theory Evolving: A Problem-Centered Introduction to Modeling Strategic Interaction. Princeton, NJ: Princeton University Press. ISBN: 0-691-00943-0.

Ginzberg, L. (1998). The LEGENDS of the JEWS. 7 Volumes. Baltimore, MD. The Jewish Publication Society of American & Johns Hopkins University Press. ISBN: 0-8018-5891-7.

Givens, B. (1991). Son of Film Flubs. New York: Citadel Press. ISBN: 0-8065-1279-2.

Gleason, J., & Pope, W. (1990). Instructor's Resource Manual to Accompany McConnell/Brue's: Microeconomics: Principles, Problems, and Policies (11th ed.). New York: McGraw-Hill Publishing Company. ISBN: 0-07-045546-5.

Gleick, J. (1987). Chaos: Making a New Science. New York, NY: Penguin Books.

Gleick, J. (1999). Faster: The Acceleration of Just About Everything. New York: Pantheon. ISBN: 0-679-40837-1.

Glen, P. (Speaker) (1991). It's Not My Department. (Cassette Recording). New York: Simon & Schuster. ISBN: 0-671-73015-0.

Glover, D. (Host), Haffner, C., & Lusitana, D. (Producers) (1993). Civil War Journal: Stonewall Jackson/Destiny at Fort Sumter: Video 1. [Motion Picture]. United States: Greystone Communications, Inc. ISBN: 1-56501-200-3.

Glover, D. (Host), Haffner, C., & Lusitana, D. (Producers) (1993). Civil War Journal: The Monitor vs. The CSS Virginia/The Gray Ghost: John Singleton Mosby: Video 2. [Motion Picture]. United States: Greystone Communications, Inc. ISBN: 1-56501-200-3.

Glover, D. (Host), Haffner, C., & Lusitana, D. (Producers) (1993). Civil War Journal: The 54th Massachusetts/McClellan's Way: Video 3. [Motion

Picture]. United States: Greystone Communications, Inc. ISBN: 1-56501-200-3.

Glover, D. (Host), Haffner, C., & Lusitana, D. (Producers) (1993). Civil War Journal: Alexander Gardner: War Photographer/John Brown's War: Video 4. [Motion Picture]. United States: Greystone Communications, Inc. ISBN: 1-56501-200-3.

Glover, D. (Host), Haffner, C., & Lusitana, D. (Producers) (1993). Civil War Journal: The Battle of 1st Bull Run/Pickett's Charge: Video 5. [Motion Picture]. United States: Greystone Communications, Inc. ISBN: 1-56501-200-3.

Glover, D. (Host), Haffner, C., & Lusitana, D. (Producers) (1993). Civil War Journal: Days of Darkness: The Gettysburg Civilians/Banners of Glory/West Point Classmates-Civil War Enemies: Video 6. [Motion Picture]. United States: Greystone Communications, Inc. ISBN: 1-56501-200-3.

Glover, D. (Host), Haffner, C., & Lusitana, D. (Producers) (1994). Civil War Journal II: Robert E. Lee/Sherman and The March To The Sea: Video 1. [Motion Picture]. United States: Greystone Communications, Inc. ISBN: 1-56501-326-3.

Glover, D. (Host), Haffner, C., & Lusitana, D. (Producers) (1994). Civil War Journal II: General Joshua L. Chamberlain/Lincoln And Gettysburg: Video 2. [Motion Picture]. United States: Greystone Communications, Inc. ISBN: 1-56501-326-3.

Glover, D. (Host), Haffner, C., & Lusitana, D. (Producers) (1994). Civil War Journal II: The Battle of Fredericksburg/Battlefield of Medicine: Video 3. [Motion Picture]. United States: Greystone Communications, Inc. ISBN: 1-56501-326-3.

Glover, D. (Host), Haffner, C., & Lusitana, D. (Producers) (1994). Civil War Journal II: Frederick Douglass/Reporting The War: Video 4. [Motion Picture]. United States: Greystone Communications, Inc. ISBN: 1-56501-326-3.

Glover, D. (Host), Haffner, C., & Lusitana, D. (Producers) (1994). Civil War Journal II: The Battle of Chattanooga/Women at War: Video 5. [Motion Picture]. United States: Greystone Communications, Inc. ISBN: 1-56501-326-3.

Glover, D. (Host), Haffner, C., & Lusitana, D. (Producers) (1994). Civil War Journal II: Nathan Bedford Forrest/The Battle of Franklin & Nashville/Zouaves! : Video 6. [Motion Picture]. United States: Greystone Communications, Inc. ISBN: 1-56501-326-3.

Glusker, I. & Ketchum, R. with an introduction by Divine, R. (Eds.). (1971). American Testament: Fifty Great Documents of American History. New York: American Heritage Publishing Co., Inc. ISBN: 07-001138-9.

Goleman, D. (1995). Emotional Intelligence: Why it can Matter More than IQ. New York, NY: Bantam. ISBN: 0-553-09503-X.

Golenpaul, D. (Ed.). (1970). Information Please Almanac: Atlas and Yearbook (25th ed.). New York: Information Please Almanac, Atlas and Yearbook. Library of Congress Catalog Card Number: 47-845.

Good News New Testament (1976). Good News New Testament (4th ed.). New York: American Bible Society.

Goodwin, H. (1943). Aerial Warfare: The Story of the Aeroplane as a Weapon. New York: The New Home Library.

Gordon, S., Gordon, F., Fusaro, B.A., Siegel, M., & Tucker, A. (1995). Functioning in the Real World: A Precalculus Experience. Reading, MA: Addison-Wesley Publishing Company. ISBN: 0-201-84629-2.

Gore, A. (1992). Earth in the Balance: Ecology and the Human Spirit. New York: Plume: ISBN: 0-452-26935-0.

Gottheil, F. (1996). Principles of Microeconomics. Cincinnati, OH: South-Western College Publishing. ISBN: 0-538-84043-9.

Gottlieb, R. (1993). Forcing the Spring: The Transformation of the American Environmental Movement. ISBN: 1-55963-122-8.

Goulden, J. (1982). Korea: The Untold Story of the War. New York: McGraw-Hill Book Company. ISBN: 0-07-023580-5.

Govt., U.S. (2000). The Internet, Distance Learning and the Future of the Research University, Hearing before the Subcommittee on Basic Research of the Committee on Science House of Representatives, 1006th Congress Second Session. May 9, 2000. Serial No. 106-81. Coe Libr. Call #: Y 4.sci 2:106-81 (basement Coe).

Gowdy, C. (1993). Seasons to Remember: The Way It Was in American Sports 1945-1960. New York: HarperCollins.

Graham, B. & Dodd, D. (1934). Security Analysis. New York: McGraw-Hill Book Company, Inc. ISBN: 0-07-024496-0.

Graves, P. (Speaker) (1988). Alaska, by James A. Michener. (Cassette Recording). New York: Random House. ISBN: 0-394-57078-2.

Gray, J. (1998). False Dawn. New York: The New Press.

Green, J. & Lewis, D. (1983). Know Your Own Mind. New York: Rawson Associates. ISBN: 0-89256-268-4.

Greene, W. (1997). Econometric Analysis (3rd ed.). Upper Saddle River, NJ: Prentice Hall. ISBN: 0-02-346602-2.

Greider, W. (1987). Secrets of the Temple: How the Federal Reserve Runs the Country. New York, NY: A Touchstone Book. ISBN: 0-671-67556-7.

Greider, W. (1997). One World, Ready or Not: The Manic Logic of Global Capitalism. New York: Simon & Schuster. ISBN: 0-64-81141-3.

Griffeth, B. (1995). The Mutual Fund Masters: A Revealing Look Into the Minds & Strategies of Wall Street's Best & Brightest. Chicago, IL: Probus Publishing. ISBN: 1-55738-582-3.

Griffith, J. (1990). Speaker's Library of Business: Stories, Anecdotes and Humor. Englewood Cliffs, NJ: Prentice Hall. ISBN: 0-13-826975-0.

Groppelli, A.A., & Nikbakht, E. (1990). Finance (2nd ed.). New York: Barron's Educational Series, Inc. ISBN: 0-8120-4373-1.

Guiton, B. (1990). Consumer's Resource Handbook. Pueblo. CO: Government Printing Office.

Gunther, M., & Carter, B. (1988). Monday Night Mayhem: The Inside Story of ABC's Monday Night Football. New York: Beech Tree Books. ISBN: 0-688-09205-5.

Guralnik. D. (Ed.) compiled by Miller, S. (1971). Webster's New World 33,000 Word Book (2nd College ed.). New York: Simon & Schuster. ISBN: 0-671-41838-6.

Haffner, C., & Lusitana, D. (Producers) (1994). The American Revolution: Video 1: The Conflict Ignites. [Motion Picture]. United States: Greystone Communications, Inc. ISBN: 1-56501-436-7.

Haffner, C., & Lusitana, D. (Producers) (1994). The American Revolution: Video 2: 1776. [Motion Picture]. United States: Greystone Communications, Inc. ISBN: 1-56501-436-7.

Haffner, C., & Lusitana, D. (Producers) (1994). The American Revolution: Video 3: Washington and Arnold. [Motion Picture]. United States: Greystone Communications, Inc. ISBN: 1-56501-436-7.

Haffner, C., & Lusitana, D. (Producers) (1994). The American Revolution: Video 4: The World at War. [Motion Picture]. United States: Greystone Communications, Inc. ISBN: 1-56501-436-7.

Haffner, C., & Lusitana, D. (Producers) (1994). The American Revolution: Video 5: England's Last Chance. [Motion Picture]. United States: Greystone Communications, Inc. ISBN: 1-56501-436-7.

Haffner, C., & Lusitana, D. (Producers) (1994). The American Revolution: Video 6: Birth of The Republic. [Motion Picture]. United States: Greystone Communications, Inc. ISBN: 1-56501-436-7.

Haggarty, J., with an introduction by Rogge, B. (Ed.). (1976). The Wisdom of Adam Smith: A Collection of His Most Incisive and Eloquent Observations. Indianapolis, IN: Liberty Press. ISBN: 0-913966-22-3.

Hailstones, T., & Mastrianna, F. (1991). Contemporary Economic Problems and Issues (9th ed.). Cincinnati, OH: College Division-South-Western Publishing Co. ISBN: 0-538-80948-5.

Haines, C. (1992). Student Solutions Manual to accompany: Elementary Differential Equations & Boundary Value Problems. New York: John Wiley & Sons, Inc. ISBN: 0-471-55127-9.

Halberstam, D. (1993). The Fifties. New York: Villard Books. ISBN: 0-679-41559-9.

Hales, P. (1997). Atomic Spaces: Living on the Manhattan Project. Urbana, IL: University of Illinois Press. ISBN: 0-252-02296-3.

Haley, A. (1976). Roots: The Saga of an American Family. New York, NY: Dell Publishing. ISBN: 0-440-17464-3.

Hall, R., & Taylor, J. (1993). Macro Economics (4th ed.). New York: W.W. Norton & Company. ISBN: 0-393-96307-1.

Halpern, H. (Speaker) (1987). Break Your Addiction to a Person. (Cassette Recording). New York: Bantam Audio Publishing. ISBN: 0-553-45047-6.

Halttunen, K. (1998). Murder Most Foul: The Killer and the American Gothic Imagination. Cambridge, MA: Harvard University Press. ISBN: 0-674-58855-X.

Hammond, J. (1999). Conversations with Great Thinkers: The Classics for People too Busy to Read Them. Providence, RI: Noontide Press. ISBN: 1-57502-598-1.

Hancock, R., & Ashton, E. (1989). Earn Money Reading Books. U.S.A.: Broughton Hall, Inc. ISBN: 0-934748-31-4.

Hanley, N., Shogren, J., & White, B. (1997). Environmental Economics in Theory and Practice. New York: Oxford University Press. ISBN: 0-19-521255-X.

Hanson, N.E. (1987). How You Can Make $25,000 a Year Writing (No Matter Where You Live) (2nd ed.). Cincinnati, OH: Writer's Digest Books.

Harkness, J. (1994). The Academy Awards Handbook: Who Won What When? (1994 ed.). New York: Pinnacle Books.

Harris, J. (1998). Curriculum-Based Telecollaboration: Using Activity Structures to Design Student Projects, *Learning & Leading With Technology.* Vol. 26. Number 1. September 1998. Pp. 6-15.

Harris, S. (Publisher) (1988). Harris' Farmer's Almanac (1989 ed.). Sharon, CT: Harris' Farmers' Almanac.

Harris, T. (1988). The Silence of the Lambs. New York: St. Martin's Paperbacks. ISBN: 0-312-92458-5.

Hart, W. (1951). College Trigonometry. Boston, MA: D.C. Heath and Company.

Hartley, R. (1992). Marketing Mistakes (5th ed.). New York: John Wiley & Sons, Inc. ISBN: 0-471-54836-7.

Hartman, G. (1991). How to Negotiate a Bigger Raise. New York: Barron's Educational Series, Inc. ISBN: 0-8120-4604-8.

Harvey, D. (1996). Justice, Nature & the Geography of Difference. Malden, MA: Blackwell Publishers. ISBN: 1-55786-681-3.

Hawking, S. (1988). A Brief History of Time: From the Big Bang to Black Holes. New York, NY: Bantam Books. ISBN: 0-553-34614-8.

Hawking, S., & Penrose, R. (1996). The Nature of Space and Time. Princeton, NJ: Princeton University Press. ISBN: 0-691-03791-4.

Hayden, D. (1995). The Power of Place: Urban Landscapes as Public History. Cambridge, MA: The MIT Press. ISBN: 0-262-58152-3.

Heath, G. (1989). Doing Business with Banks. Denver, CO: United Banks of Colorado, Inc. ISBN: 0-9623881-0-6.

Heath, T.L. (translator) (1956). Euclid: The Thirteen Books of The Elements (2nd ed., Rev.). Vol. 1 (Books I and II). New York: Dover Publications. ISBN: 0-486-60088-2.

Heath, T.L. (translator) (1956). Euclid: The Thirteen Books of The Elements (2nd ed., Rev.). Vol. 2 (Books III-IX). New York: Dover Publications, Inc. ISBN: 0-486-60089-0.

Heath, T.L. (translator) (1956). Euclid: The Thirteen Books of The Elements (2nd ed., Rev.). Vol. 3 (Books X-XIII). New York: Dover Publications, Inc. ISBN: 0-486-60090-4.

Heffner, R. (Ed.). (1984). Democracy in America: Alexis de Tocqueville. New York: The Penguin Group. Library of Congress Catalog Card Number: 56-7402.

Hegland, K. (2000). Introduction to The Study and Practice of Law. St. Paul, MN: West Group.

Heilbroner, R. (1999). The Worldly Philosophers: The Lives, Times, and Ideas of the Great Economic Thinkers. New York, NY: A Touchstone Book Published by Simon & Schuster. ISBN: 0-684-86214-X

Heilbroner, R., & Thurow, L. (1981). Five Economic Challenges. Englewood Cliffs, NJ: Prentice-Hall, Inc. ISBN: 0-13-321109-6.

Hein, J. (1996). Discrete Mathematics. Sudbury, MA: Jones and Bartlett Publishers. ISBN: 0-86720-496-6.

Hemmingway, E. (1987) Winner Take Nothing. New York, NY: Collier Books. ISBN: 0-02-051820-X.

Hempel, G., Coleman, A., & Simonson, D. (1986). Bank Management: Text and Cases. New York: John Wiley & Sons. ISBN: 0-471-82147-0.

Henderson, J., & Quandt, R. (1980). <u>Microeconomic Theory: A Mathematical Approach</u> (3rd ed.). New York: McGraw-Hill, Inc. ISBN: 0-07-028101-7.

Henslin, J. (1988). <u>Down To Earth Sociology: Introductory Readings</u> (5th ed.). New York: The Free Press. ISBN: 0-02-914451-5.

Herzog, Y.D. (1980). <u>The Mishnah: Berakoth, Peah, & Demai</u> (2nd ed.). London: The Soncino Press. ISBN: 0-900689-18-8.

Hilgard, E., Atkinson, R., & Atkinson, R. (1979). <u>Introduction to Psychology</u> (7th ed.). New York: Harcourt Brace Jovanovich, Inc. ISBN: 0-15-543668-6.

Hill, N. (1963). <u>Think & Grow Rich.</u> New York: Faucett Crest. ISBN: 0-449-20365-4.

Hinchman, H. (1991). <u>A Life in Hand: Creating The Illuminated Journal.</u> Salt Lake City, UT: Peregrine Smith Books. ISBN: 0-87905-380-1.

Hitler, A. translated by Manheim, R. (1971). <u>Mein Kamph.</u> Boston, MA: Houghton Mifflin. ISBN: 0-395-08362-1.

Hobbes, T. (1985). <u>Leviathan.</u> London, England: Penguin Books. ISBN: 0-14-043195.

Hobsbawm, E. (1990). <u>Nations and Nationalism Since 1780: Programme, Myth, and Reality.</u> Cambridge: Cambridge University Press.

Hobsbawm, E., & Ranger, T. (Eds.). (1983). <u>The Invention of Tradition.</u> Cambridge: Cambridge University Press. ISBN: 0-521-43773-3.

Hoffman, M., Foley, J., & McGuire, T. (Eds.). (1988). <u>The World Almanac and Book of Facts.</u> (1989 ed.). New York: World Almanac. ISBN: 0-88687-361-4.

Hoffman, M., Foley, J., & McGuire, T. (Eds.). (1990). <u>The World Almanac and Book of Facts.</u> (1991 ed.). New York: World Almanac. ISBN: 0-88687-578-1.

Holland, J. (1998). <u>Emergence: From Chaos to Order.</u> Cambridge, MA: Perseus Books. ISBN: 0-201-14943-5.

Howells, J., & Merwin, D. (1985). <u>Choose Mexico.</u> San Francisco, CA: Gateway Books. ISBN: 0-933469-00-4.

Hubbard, R. (2000). <u>Battlefield Earth.</u> Los Angeles, CA: Bridge Audio. ISBN: 0-88404-682-6.

Hufford, M. (1992). <u>Chaseworld: Foxhunting and Storytelling in New Jersey's Pine Barrens.</u> Philadelphia: University of Pennsylvania Press.

Hummel, R. (1985). <u>Electronic Properties of Materials: An Introduction for Engineers.</u> New York: Springer-Verlag. ISBN: 0-387-15631-3.

Hunger, B. (1992). <u>Hiking Wyoming.</u> Helena, MT: Falcon Press Publishing Co. ISBN: 1-56044-506-8.

Hutchins, Robert M. (1952). <u>The Great Conversation: The Substance of a Liberal Education.</u> 54 Volumes. Eds. Mortimer J. Adler. Chicago, IL: William Benton & Encyclopedia Britannica, Inc.

Iacocca, L., with Novak, W. (1984). Iacocca: An Autobiography. New York, NY: Bantam Books. ISBN: 0-553-05067-2.
Ignatiev, N. (1995). How the Irish Became White. NY: Routledge. ISBN: 0-415-91384-5.
Impe, J.V., with Campbell, R. (1979). Israel's Final Holocaust. Nashville, TN: Thomas Nelson Publishers. ISBN: 0-8407-9005-8.
Intel. (1979). 8080/8085 Assembly Language Programming. Santa Clara, CA: Intel Literature Sales.
Intel. (1983). The NCS 80/85 User's Manual. Santa Clara, CA: Intel Literature Sales.
Intel. (1987). 80386 Hardware Reference Manual. Santa Clara, CA: Intel Literature Sales.
Isbister, J. (1998). Promises not Kept: The Betrayal of Social Change in the Third World. West Hartford, CT: Kumarian Press. ISBN: 1-56549-078-9.
Itkoff, S., & Taplin, J. (Executive Producers), Based on the Book *Last Oasis* by Sandra Postel (1997). Cadillac Desert: Last Oasis, Program 4. [Motion Picture]. United States: Trans Pacific Television. ISBN: 0-7800-1926-1.
Itkoff, S., Taplin, J. (Executive Producers), & Else, J. (Writer/Producer) (1997). Cadillac Desert: Mulhulholland's Dream, Program 1. [Motion Picture]. United States: Trans Pacific Television. ISBN: 0-7800-1926-1.
Itkoff, S., Taplin, J. (Executive Producers), & Else, J. (Writer/Producer) (1997). Cadillac Desert: An American Nile, Program 2. [Motion Picture]. United States: Trans Pacific Television. ISBN: 0-7800-1926-1.
Itkoff, S., Taplin, J. (Executive Producers), & Else, J. (Writer/Producer) (1997). Cadillac Desert: The Mercy of Nature, Program 3. [Motion Picture]. United States: Trans Pacific Television. ISBN: 0-7800-1926-1.
Jackle, J., & Sculle, K. (1999). Fast Food: Roadside Restaurants in the Automobile Age. Baltimore, MD: The Johns Hopkins University Press. ISBN: 0-8018-6109-8.
Jacob, H. (1984). Justice in America (4th ed.). Boston, MA: Little, Brown and Company. ISBN: 0-316-45532-6.
Jacobs, L. (1984). The Talmudic Argument: A Study in Talmudic Reasoning and Methodology. London, England: Cambridge University Press. Coe Library Call #: BM 503.7.J33 1985. ISBN: 0-521-26370-0.
Jacquot, R., & Long, F. Introduction to Engineering Systems. Laramie, WY: Department of Electrical Engineering at the University of Wyoming.
Jaffe, W. (Trans.) (1977). Elements of Pure Economics or The Theory of Social Wealth. (Walras, L., Author). Fairfield, NJ: Agustus M. Kelley, Publishers. ISBN: 0-678-06028-2.
James, K. (1994). Holy Bible. U.S.A.: Thomas Nelson Publishers.

James, W. (1918). <u>The Principles of Psychology.</u> Vol. I & II. New York, NY: Dover Publications, Inc. ISBN: 0-486-20381-6.

Janeway, E. (1989). <u>The Economics of Chaos: On Revitalizing the American Economy.</u> New York: Truman Talley Books; E.P. Dutton. ISBN: 0-525-24711-4.

Jansen, J.S. (1990). <u>City of Laramie, Wyoming: Its Resources.</u> Board of Trade.

Jaspers, K. (1957). <u>Socrates, Buddah, Confucius, Jesus.</u> San Diego, CA: Harcourt Brace Jovanovich, Publishers. ISBN: 0-15-683580-0.

Jeffers, S. (1991). <u>Brother Eagle, Sister Sky: A message from Chief Seattle.</u> New York, NY: Dial Books. ISBN: 0-8037-0969-2.

Jenkins, M., Ringel, J. & Romberg, G. (1989). <u>Starting and Operating a Business in Colorado</u> (2nd ed.). Grants Pass, OR: Oasis Press. ISBN: 0-916378-52-7.

Jessup. P. (1980). <u>Modern Bank Management.</u> St. Paul, MN: West Publishing Company. ISBN: 0-8299-0330-5.

Jevons, W. (1931). <u>The Theory of Political Economy</u> (4th ed.). London, England: MacMillan & Co.

Johnson, J. and Hinton, E. (1993). <u>Turning the Thing Around: Pulling America's Team out of the Dumps-and Myself out of the Doghouse.</u> New York, NY: Hyperion. ISBN: 1-56282-725-1.

Johnston, B. (Ed.). (1982). <u>My Inventions: The Autobiography of Nikola Tesla.</u> New York: Barnes & Noble Books. ISBN: 0-76070-085-0.

Josephy, A. (1993). <u>The Native Americans: An Illustrated History.</u> Atlanta, GA: Turner Publishing, Inc. ISBN: 1-878685-42-2.

Joyce, J. (1990). <u>Ulysses.</u> New York, NY: Vintage. ISBN: 0-679-72276-9.

Jurgensen, R., Donnelly, A., & Dolciani, M. (1965). <u>Modern Geometry: Structure and Method.</u> Boston, MA: Houghton Mifflin Company.

Kadushin, M. (1969). <u>A Conceptual Approach to the Mekilta.</u> New York: The Jewish Theological Seminary of America.

Kadushin, M. (1969). <u>A Conceptual Approach to the Mekilta.</u> New York: The Jewish Theological Seminary of America.

Kafka, F. (1984). <u>The Trial.</u> New York: Schocken Books. ISBN: 0-8052-0848-8.

Kalat, J. (1996). <u>Introduction to Psychology</u> (4th ed.). Pacific Grove, CA: Brooks/Cole Publishing Company. ISBN: 0-534-25014-9.

Kalat, J. (1996). <u>Introduction to Psychology</u> (4th ed.). Pacific Grove, CA: Brooks/Cole Publishing Company. ISBN: 0-534-25014-9.

Katz, M., & Rosen, H. (1994). <u>Microeconomics</u> (2nd ed.). Burr Ridge, IL: Irwin. ISBN: 0-256-11171-5.

Katz, R., & Oblinger, D. (Eds.). (2000). <u>The 'E' is for Everything: E-Commerce, E-Business, and E-Learning in the Future of Higher Education.</u> San

Francisco, CA: Jossey-Bass Inc. Coe Libr. Call #: LB 2395.7.E58 2000. 0-7879-5010-6.

Katzman, D., Yetman, N., & Graebner, W. (Eds.). (1997). American Studies: From Culture Concept to Cultural Studies. American Studies, Vol.38 (2). ISSN: 0026-3079.

Katzman, D., Yetman, N., & Graebner, W. (Eds.). (1998). TV and American Culture. American Studies, Vol. 39(#2). ISSN: 0026-3079.

Katzman, D., Yetman, N., & Graebner, W. (Eds.). (1999). American Studies: A Critical Retrospective. American Studies, Vol. 40(#2). ISSN: 0026-3079.

Katzman, D., Yetman, N., & Graebner, W. (Eds.). (2000). Globalization, Transnationalism, and The End of the American Century. American Studies, Vol. 41(#2/3). ISSN: 0026-3079.

Katzman, D., Yetman, N., & Graebner, W. (Eds.). (2000). The National Geographic Magazine. American Studies, Vol. 41 (#1). ISSN: 0026-3079.

Kaufman, G. (1975). Money and the Financial System: Fundamentals. Chicago, IL: Rand McNally College Publishing Company. Library of Congress Catalog Card Number: 74-19514.

Kaufman, P., & Corrigan, A. (1986). The New Tax Law and What It Means To You. Stamford, CT: LongMeadow Press. ISBN: 0-681-40184-2.

Kaufmann, J. (1981). Mathematics Is...(2nd ed.). Boston, MA: Prindle, Weber & Schmidt. ISBN: 0-87150-313-1.

Kaufmann, W. (Translator) (1961). Goethe's Faust. New York: Anchor Books. ISBN: 0-385-03114-9.

Kearsley, Greg. (2000). Online Education: Learning and Teaching in Cyberspace. Toronto, Canada: Wadsworth. Coe Libr. Call #: LB 1028.5.K35 2000. ISBN: 0-534-50689-5. [Also On-line]. Available: http://home.sprynet.com/~gkearsley/cyber.htm.

Keillor, G. (Speaker) (1989). More News From Lake Wobegon: Faith. (Cassette Recording). St Paul, MN: Minnesota Public Radio. ISBN: 0-942110-30-7.

Keillor, G. (Speaker) (1989). More News From Lake Wobegon: Hope. (Cassette Recording). St Paul, MN: Minnesota Public Radio. ISBN: 0-942110-30-7.

Keillor, G. (Speaker) (1989). More News From Lake Wobegon: Humor. (Cassette Recording). St Paul, MN: Minnesota Public Radio. ISBN: 0-942110-30-7.

Keillor, G. (Speaker) (1989). More News From Lake Wobegon: Love. (Cassette Recording). St Paul, MN: Minnesota Public Radio. ISBN: 0-942110-30-7.

Kelchner, J. (1940). The Bible and King Solomon's Temple in Masonry. Philadelphia, PA: A. J. Holman Company.

Kelly, K., Nizer, L., Clurman, R., & Greene, M. Today's Best Nonfiction. Pleasantville, NY: Reader's Digest.

Kemmis, D. (1990). <u>Community and the Politics of Place</u>. Norman, OK: University of Oklahoma Press. ISBN: 0-8061-2477-6.

Kennedy, P. (1987). <u>Economic Change and Military Conflict from 1500-2000: The Rise and Fall of the Great Powers.</u> New York: Random House.

Kenrick, D., Neuberg, S., & Cialdini, R. (2002). <u>Social Psychology: Unraveling the Mystery</u> (2nd ed.). Boston, MA: Allyn and Bacon. ISBN: 0-205-33297-8.

Kent, P. (1996). <u>The Complete Idiot's Guide to the Internet</u> (3rd ed.). Indianapolis, IN: QUE, A division of Macmillan Computer Publishing. ISBN: 0-7897-0862-0.

Keown, A., Scott, A., Jr., Martin, J., & Petty, J.W. (1985). <u>Basic Financial Management.</u> (3rd ed.). Englewood Cliffs, NJ: Prentice Hall. ISBN: 0-13-060641-3.

Keown, A., Scott, A., Jr., Martin, J., & Petty, J.W. (1994). <u>Foundations of Finance: The Logic and Practice of Financial Management.</u> Englewood Cliffs, NJ: Prentice Hall. ISBN: 0-13-211087-3.

Kerasote, T. (1993). <u>Bloodties: Nature, Culture, and the Hunt.</u> New York: Random House.

Kershul, K. (1982). <u>Japanese in 10 Minutes a Day.</u> Seattle, WA: Bilingual Books, Inc. ISBN: 0-916682-92-7.

Keynes, J. (1953). <u>The General Theory of Employment, Interest, and Money.</u> Orlando, FL: A Harvest Book. ISBN: 0-15-634711-3.

Keynes, J. (1997). <u>The General Theory of Employment, Interest, and Money.</u> Amherst, NY: Prometheus Books. ISBN: 1-57392-139-4.

Kilpatrick, A. (1994). <u>Of Permanent Value: The Story of Warren Buffett.</u> Birmingham, AL: AKPE. ISBN: 0-9641905-0-8.

King, Larry with Peter Occhiogrosso. (1988). <u>Tell it to the King</u>. New York, NY. G.P. Putnam's Sons. ISBN: 0-399-13244-9.

King, S. (1978). <u>The Stand.</u> New York: A Signet Book.

King, S. (1993). <u>Nightmares & Dreamscapes.</u> New York: Viking. ISBN: 0-670-85108-6.

King, S. (1994). <u>Insomnia.</u> New York: Viking. ISBN: 0-670-85503-0.

Kinoshita, S. (1994). <u>Directory of Companies Offering Dividend Reinvestment Plans</u> (11th ed.). Laurel, MD: Evergreen Enterprises. ISBN: 0-933183-15-1.

Kittel, Hoffer, & Wright (1989). <u>Biblical Hebrew: A Text and Workbook</u> (Cassette Recording, Tape 1). Yale University Press. ISBN: 0-300-04395-3.

Klott, G. (1987). <u>The New York Times Complete Guide to Personal Investing.</u> New York: Times Books. ISBN: 0-8129-1235-7.

Kluger, R. (1975). <u>Simple Justice: The history of Brown v. Board of Education, the epochal Supreme Court decision that outlawed segregation, and of black</u>

America's century-long struggle for equality under law. New York, NY: Vintage Books. ISBN: 0-394-72255-8.

Knobloch, F. (1996). The Culture of Wilderness. Chapel Hill: University of North Carolina Press. ISBN: 0-8078-2280-9.

Knobloch, F. (1996). The Culture of Wilderness: Agriculture as Colonization in the American West. Chapel Hill, NC. The University of North Carolina Press. ISBN: 0-8078-4585-X.

Knowles, R.S. (1959). The Greatest Gamblers: The Epic of American Oil Exploration. Norman, OK. University of Oklahoma Press. ISBN: 0-8061-1654-4.

Komroff, M. (Ed.). (1992). The Apocrypha. New York: Barnes & Noble Books. ISBN:0-88029-991-6.

Kopple, B. (Producer). (1976). Harlan County USA. [Motion Picture]. (Available from First Run Features, 153 Waverly Place, New York, NY, 10014)

Kreinin, M. (1998). International Economics, A Policy Approach: Euro Update (8th ed.). Orlando, FL: The Dryden Press. ISBN: 0-03-045242-2.

Kreps, D. (1988). Notes on the Theory of Choice. Boulder, CO: Westview Press. ISBN: 0-8133-7553-3.

Kreps, D. (1990). A Course in Microeconomic Theory. Princeton, NJ: Princeton University Press. ISBN: 0-691-04264-0.

Kreps, D. (1990). Game Theory and Economic Modelling. New York: Oxford University Press. ISBN: 0-19-828357-1.

Krugman, P., & Obstfeld, M. (1997). International Economics: Theory and Policy (4th ed.). Reading, MA: Addison-Wesley, Inc. ISBN: 0-673-52497-3.

Krugman, Paul. (1994). The Age of Diminished Expectations. Cambridge, MA. The MIT Press. ISBN: 0-262-61092-2.

Krugman, Paul. (1999). The Return of Depression Economics. New York, NY: W.W. Norton & Company. ISBN: 0-393-04839-X.

Kuhn, Harold (Ed.). (1997). Classics in Game Theory. Princeton, NJ: Princeton University Press. ISBN: 0-691-01192-3.

Kuhn, T. (1996). The Structure of Scientific Revolutions (3rd ed.). Chicago, IL: University of Chicago Press. ISBN: 0-226-45808-3.

Labaton, A. (Executive Producer) (1998). HERITAGE: Civilization and the Jews, A People is Born & The Power of the World. Vol 1 of 5 [VHS Documentary Video]. New York: Home Vision Entertainment.

Labaton, A. (Executive Producer) (1998). HERITAGE: Civilization and the Jews, The Shaping of Traditions & The Crucible of Europe. Vol 2 of 5 [VHS Documentary Video]. New York: Home Vision Entertainment.

Labaton, A. (Executive Producer) (1998). HERITAGE: Civilization and the Jews, The Search for Deliverance & Roads from the Ghetto. Vol 3 of 5 [VHS Documentary Video]. New York: Home Vision Entertainment.

Labaton, A. (Executive Producer) (1998). HERITAGE: Civilization and the Jews, The Golden Land & Out of the Ashes. Vol 4 of 5 [VHS Documentary Video]. New York: Home Vision Entertainment.

Labaton, A. (Executive Producer) (1998). HERITAGE: Civilization and the Jews, Into the Future. Vol 5 of 5 [VHS Documentary Video]. New York: Home Vision Entertainment.

LaFeber, W. (1999). Michael Jordan and the New Global Capitalism. New York: W.W. Norton & Company. ISBN: 0-393-32037-5.

Landow, George P. and Paul Delany, Eds. (1993). The Digital Word: Text-Based Computing in the Humanities. Cambridge, MA: The MIT Press. Coe Libr Call #: PN 98.E4D54. ISBN: 0-262-12176-X.

Lang. S. (Speaker) (1991). The Gap into Conflict: The Real Story. (Cassette Recording) New York: Bantam Audio Publishing. ISBN: 0-553-45276-2.

Langguth, A.J. (1988). Patriots: The Men Who Started the American Revolution. New York: Simon & Schuster. ISBN: 0-671-67562-1.

Lannon, J. (1985). Technical Writing (3rd ed.). Boston, MA: Little, Brown and Company. ISBN: 0-316-51448-9.

Lapin, L. (1990). Statistics for Modern Business Decisions (5th ed.). San Diego, CA: Harcourt Brace Jovanovich. ISBN: 0-45-583705-2.

Lapp, Danielle C. (1992). Maximizing Your Memory Power. New York: Barron's. ISBN: 0-8120-4799-0.

Larson, G. (1982). The Far Side. Kansas City, KS: Andrews, McMeel & Parker. ISBN: 0-8362-1200-2.

Larson, G. (1988). Night of the Crash-Test Dummies: A Far Side Collection. Kansas City, MO: Andrews and McMeel. ISBN: 0-8362-2049-8.

Larson, T.A. (1965). History of Wyoming. Lincoln, NE: University of Nebraska Press. ISBN: 0-8032-7936-1.

Lasker, G., & Tyzzer, R. (1982). Physical Anthropology (3rd ed.). New York: Holt, Rinehart and Winston.

Laskin, D. (1986). Getting Into Advertising. New York: Ballantine Books. ISBN: 0-345-2598-2.

Lathem, E.C. (Ed.). (1969). The Poetry of Robert Frost. New York: Holt, Rinehart & Winston. Library of Congress Catalog Card Number: 68-24759.

Lawrence, T.E. (1935). Seven Pillars of Wisdom. New York: Penguin Books. ISBN: 0-14-018122-9.

Leach, W. (1999). Country of Exiles: The Destruction of Place in American Life. New York: Pantheon Books. ISBN: 0-679-44219-7.

Leathers, D. (1997). Successful Nonverbal Communication: Principles and Applications (3rd ed.). Boston, MA: Allyn and Bacon. ISBN: 0-205-26230-9.

Lee, S., & Zelenak, M. (1982). Economics for Consumers. Belmont, CA: Wadsworth Publishing Company. ISBN: 0-534-01083-0.

Lehmann, M. (1992). Real World Economic Applications: The Wall Street Journal Workbook (2nd ed.). Homewood, IL: Irwin. ISBN: 0-256-09102-1.

Lessard, B., & Baldwin, S. (2000). True Tales of Working the Web: Net Slaves. New York: Mc Graw-Hill. ISBN: 0-07-135243-0.

Letwin, G., with foreword by Gates, B. (1988). Inside OS/2. Redmond, WA: Microsoft Press. ISBN: 1-55615-117-9.

Levi, E.H. (1949). An Introduction to Legal Reasoning. Chicago, IL: The University of Chicago Press. ISBN: 0-226-47408-9.

Levin, R., & Rubin, D. (1991). Statistics for Management (5th ed.). Englewood Cliffs, NJ: Prentice Hall. ISBN: 0-13-851965-X.

Levi-Strauss, C. (1978). Myth and Meaning: Cracking the Code of Culture. New York, NY: Schocken Books. ISBN: 0-8052-1038-5.

Lewis, A. (1964). Gideon's Trumpet: How one man, a poor prisoner, took his case to the Supreme Court—and changed the law of the United States. New York, NY: Vintage Books. ISBN: 0-679-72312-9.

Lewis, J. (1975). Archaeology and the Bible. Abilene, TX: Biblical Research Press. ISBN: 0-89112-113-7.

Lewis, M. (1989). Liar's Poker. New York, NY: Penguin books. ISBN: 0-14-014345-9.

Lewis, M. (2000). The New New Thing: A Silicon Valley Story. New York: W. W. Norton and Company. ISBN: 0-393-04813-6.

Lewis, S. (1962). Babbit. New York: Signet Classics.

Limbaugh, R. (1992). The Way Things Ought to be. New York, NY: Pocket Books. ISBN: 0-671-75145-X.

Limbaugh, R. (1993). See, I Told You So. New York: Pocket Books. ISBN:0-671-87120-X.

Lindeman, J.B., & Friedman, J.P. (1995). How to Prepare for Real Estate Examinations (5th ed.). New York: Barron's Educational Series, Inc. ISBN: 0-8120-2994-1.

Linderman, F. (1957). Plenty-coups: Chief of the Crows. Lincoln, NE: University of Nebraska Press. ISBN: 0-8032-5121-1.

Lindsey, D. (1988). Microeconomics (5th ed.). Chicago, IL: The Dryden Press. ISBN: 0-03-020397-X.

Linedecker, C.L. (1993). Massacre at Waco, Texas: The Shocking True Story of Cult Leader David Koresh and the Branch Davidians. New York, NY: St. Martin's Paperbacks. ISBN: 0-312-95226-0.

Llewellyn, K. (1930). The Bramble Bush: On our Law and Its Study. New York: Oceana Publications, Inc. ISBN: 0-379-00073-3.

Loewen, J.W. (1999) Lies Across America: What our Historic Sites Get Wrong. New York, NY: Touchstone & Simon and Schuster. ISBN: 0-684-87067-3.

Loewen, J.W. (1999). Lies Across America: What Our Historic Sites Get Wrong. New York: Touchstone. ISBN: 0-684-87067-3.

London, J. (1993). The Call of the Wild. U.S.A.: Watermill Press. ISBN: 0-8167-2881-X.

Long, F.M., & Lonsdale, E.M. (1981). Introductory Electrical Concepts. Laramie, WY: Electrical Engineering Department at the University of Wyoming.

Loomis, L. (1974). Calculus (3rd ed.). Reading, MA: Addison-Wesley Publishing Company. ISBN: 0-201-05045-5.

Lott, Eric. (1995). Love & Theft: Blackface Minstrelsy and the American Working Class. New York, New York: Oxford University Press. ISBN: 0-19-509641-X.

Lowi, T., & Ginsberg, B. (1990). American Government: Freedom and Power. New York: W.W. Norton & Company. ISBN: 0-393-95699-7.

Ludlum, R. (1979). The Holcroft Covenant. New York: Bantam Books. ISBN: 0-553-20783-0.

Ludlum, R. (1986). The Bourne Supremacy. New York: Bantam Books. ISBN: 0-553-26322-6.

Ludlum, R. (1988). The Icarus Agenda. New York: Bantam Books. ISBN: 0-553-57800-2.

Lujan, M., & Snyder. H. (1993). Surface Coal Mining Reclamation: 15 Years of Progress, 1977-1992. Washington, D.C.: United States Department of the Interior.

Lundlum, R. (1973). Trevayne. New York: Bantam Books. ISBN: 0-553-28179-8.

Luttwak, E. (1999). Turbo Capitalism: Winners and Losers in the Global Economy. New York: HarperCollins. ISBN: 0-06-019330-1.

Lynch, P., & Rothchild, J. (1989). One up on Wall Street: How to Use What You Already Know to Make Money in the Market. New York, NY: Penguin Books. ISBN: 0-14-012792-5.

Lynch, P., & Rothchild, J. (1993). Beating the Street. New York, NY: Simon & Schuster. ISBN: 0-671-75915-9.

Lynch, P., & Rothchild, J. (1995). Learn to Earn: A Beginner's Guide to the Basics of Investing and Business. New York, NY: A Fireside Book. ISBN: 0-684-81163-4.

Macdonald, A. (1980). The Turner Diaries (2nd ed.). New York: Barricade Books, Inc. ISBN: 1-56980-086-3.

MacGregor, M. (1980). Training Your Children to Handle Money. Minneapolis, MN: Bethany Fellowship Inc. ISBN: 0-87123-540-4.

Mackay, H. (1990). Beware the Naked Man Who Offers You His Shirt. New York: Ivy Books. ISBN: 0-8041-0583-9.

MacKillop, J., & Cross, D. (1978). Speaking of Words: A Language Reader. New York: Holt, Rinehart and Winston. ISBN: 0-03-018056-2.

MacKinnon, C. (1984). Scottish Highlanders. New York: Barnes & Noble Books. ISBN: 0-88029-950-9.

MacNicol, P. (Speaker) (1990). Nemesis, by Isaac Asimov. (Cassette Recording). New York: Bantam Audio Publishing. ISBN: 0-553-45235-5.

Madden, J, with Anderson, D. (1996). All Madden: Hey, I'm Talking Pro Football. New York, NY: HarperCollins Publishers. ISBN: 0-06-017205-3.

Madden, J. (1988). The First Book of Football. New York, NY: Crown Publishers, Inc. ISBN: 0-517-58593-6.

Maddox, L. (Ed.). (December 2000). American Quarterly, Vol. 52(#4). ISSN: 0003-0678.

Maddox, L. (Ed.). (June 2000). American Quarterly, Vol. 52(#2). ISSN: 0003-0678.

Maddox, L. (Ed.). (June 2001). American Quarterly, Vol. 53(#2). ISSN: 0003-0678.

Maddox, L. (Ed.). (March 2000). American Quarterly, Vol. 52(#1). ISSN: 0003-0678.

Maddox, L. (Ed.). (March 2001). American Quarterly, Vol. 53(#1). ISSN: 0003-0678.

Maddox, L. (Ed.). (September 2000). American Quarterly, Vol. 52(#3). ISSN: 0003-0678.

Maddox, L. (Ed.). (September 2001). American Quarterly, Vol. 53(#3). ISSN: 0003-0678.

Maginn, J., & Tuttle, D. (Eds.). (1983). Managing Investment Portfolios: A Dynamic Process. Boston, MA: Warren, Gorham & Lamont. ISBN: 0-88262-874-7.

Maimonides, M. (1956). The Guide for the Perplexed (2nd ed.). New York: Dover Publications, Inc..

Malburg, C. (1991). How to Fire your Boss. New York: Berkley Books. ISBN:0-425-12734-6.

Malina, R. (1996). Program for Athletic Coaches' Education: Reference Manual & Study Guide. Carmel, IN: Cooper Publishing Group. ISBN: 1-884125-52-2.

Malone, R. (1992). You're Not Alone: Daily Encouragement For Those Looking For A New Job. Nashville: Thomas Nelson Publishers.

Malthus, T.R. (1798). An Essay on the Principle of Population. Oxford: Oxford University Press. ISBN: 0-19-283096-1.

Maltin, L. (1989). Leonard Maltin's TV Movies and Video Guide (1990 ed.). New York: Signet.

Maltin, L. (1992). Leonard Maltin's Movie and Video Guide, 1994. New York: Signet.

Mander, J., & Goldsmith, E. (Eds.). (1996). The Case Against the Global Economy and For a Turn Toward the Local. San Francisco, CA: Sierra Club Books. ISBN: 0-87156-865-9.

Mankiw, G. (1992). Macroeconomics. New York: Worth Publishers. ISBN: 0-87901-502-0.

Mano, M. M. (1984). Digital Design. Englewood Cliffs, NJ: Prentice-Hall, Inc. ISBN: 0-13-212333-9.

Mansfield, E. (1985). Micro-Economics: Theory and Applications (5th ed.). New York: W.W. Norton & Company. ISBN: 0-393-95397-1.

Mansfield, E., & Behravesh, N. (1995). Economics USA (4th ed.). New York: W.W. Norton & Company. ISBN: 0-393-96641-0.

Marshall, A. (1997). Principles of Economics. New York: Prometheus Books. ISBN: 1-57392-140-8.

Marshall, S.L.A. (1956). Pork Chop Hill. New York: Jove Books. ISBN: 0-515-08732-7.

Martin, J., Petty, J.W., Keown, A., & Scott, D. Jr. (1991). Basic Financial Management (5th ed.). Englewood Cliffs, NJ: Prentice-Hall Inc. ISBN: 0-13-060807-6.

Martin, J., Petty, W., Keown, A., & Scott, D. Jr. (1991). Basic Financial Management (5th ed.). Englewood Cliffs, NJ: Prentice Hall, Inc. ISBN: 0-13-060856-4.

Martin, M., & Porter, M. (1989). Video Movie Guide, 1990. New York: Ballantine Books. ISBN: 0-345-36329-9.

Martin, M., & Porter, M. (1999). Video Movie Guide, 2000. New York: Ballantine Books. ISBN: 0-345-43957-0.

Marx, K., introduced by Mandel, E. and Translated by Fowkes, B. (1976). Capital: A Critique of Political Economy. New York: Vintage Books. ISBN: 0-394-72657-X.

Marx, K., introduced by Mandel, E. and Translated by Fowkes, B. (1976). Capital: A Critique of Political Economy. New York: Vintage Books. ISBN: 0-394-72657-X.

Marx, L. (1964). The Machine in the Garden: Technology and the Pastoral Ideal in America. New York, NY: Oxford University Press. ISBN: 0-19-500738-7.

Mas-Colell, A., & Whinston, M. (1995). Microeconomic Theory. New York: Oxford University Press. ISBN: 0-19-510268-1.

Massachusetts Institute of Technology. (2001). MIT to make nearly all course materials available free on the World Wide Web. [On-line]. Available: http://web.mit.edu/newsoffice/nr/2001/ocw.html. April 4, 2001.

Massey, G. (Ed.). (1996). Readings for Sociology (2nd ed.). New York: W.W. Norton. ISBN: 0-393-96869-3.

Master Publishing, Inc. (1984). Dictionary of Microcomputer Terms with Illustrations. Dallas, TX: Master Publishing, Inc.

Master Publishing, Inc. (1987). The Technology Dictionary with Illustrations. Dallas, TX: Master Publishing, Inc.

Matlin, M. (1988). Sensation and Perception (2nd ed.). Needham Heights, MA: Allyn and Bacon, Inc. ISBN: 0-25-11125-4.

Maxwell, R. (Writer), & Moctesuma Esparza, R.K. (Producer). (1993). Gettysburg. [Motion Picture]. United States: Turner Home Entertainment. ISBN: 0-7806-0386-9.

Mayer, J.P. (Ed.) with a translation by Lawrence, G. (1969). Democracy in America. Alexis De Tocqueville, (author). Garden City, NY: Doubleday & Company, Inc.

McConnell, C., & Brue, S. (1990). Microeconomics: Principles, Problems, and Policies. New York: McGraw-Hill Publishing Company. ISBN: 0-07-045522-8.

McConnell, C., & Brue, S. (1990). Test Bank I to accompany Microeconomics: Principles, Problems, and Policies. New York: McGraw-Hill Publishing Company. ISBN: 0-07-045545-7.

McConnell, C.R. (1972). Economics: Principles, Problems, and Policies (5th ed.). New York: McGraw-Hill Book Company. ISBN: 07-044893-0.

McCullough, D. (1992). Truman. New York, NY: A Touchstone Book. ISBN: 0-671-86920-5.

McDonough, W., Mishkin, F., & Posen, A. (August 1997). Special Issue on Inflation Targeting. Federal Reserve Bank of New York's Economic Policy Review, Vol. 3(#3). ISBN: 0-321-03132-6.

McDowall, R. (Speaker) (1988). Transformation: The Breakthrough, by Whitley Strieber. (Cassette Recording). Studio City, CA: Dove/William Morrow Books on Tape, Inc. ISBN: 1-55800-103-4.

McGinniss, J. (1983). Fatal Vision. New York: Signet. ISBN: 0-451-16566-7.

McHugh, T. (1972). The Time of the Buffalo. New York, NY: Knopf. ISBN: 0-8032-8105-6.

McMichael, P. (1996). Development and Social Change: A Global Perspective. Thousand Oaks, CA: Pine Forge Press. ISBN: 0-8039-9066-9.

McPhee, J. (1969). <u>Levels of the Game.</u> New York: The Noonday Press of Farrar, Straus, & Giroux.

McPhee, J. (1999). <u>A Sense of Where you are: A Profile of Bill Bradley at Princeton.</u> New York: The Noonday Press of Farrar, Straus, Giroux.

McPherson, J. (1988). <u>Battle Cry of Freedom: The Civil War Era.</u> New York: Ballantine Books. ISBN: 0-345-35942-9.

McRaney, G. (Speaker) (1991). <u>Battleground by W.E.B. Griffin.</u> (Cassette Recording). New York: Simon & Schuster. ISBN: 0-671-73005-3.

McWhirter, N. (1980). <u>Guinness Book of World Records</u> (19th ed.). New York: Bantam Books. ISBN: 0-553-14500-2.

Means, R., with Wolf, M.J. (1995). <u>Where White Men Fear to Tread: the Autobiography of Russell Means.</u> San Bruno, CA: Audio Literature. ISBN: 1-57453-011-9.

Mechling, Jay. (1997). Some New Elementary Axioms For An American Cultural Studies. *American Studies.* Vol. 38.

Meier, P., Minirth, F., & Wichern, F. (1982). <u>Introduction to Psychology & Counseling: Christian Perspectives & Applications.</u> Grand Rapids, MI: Baker Book House. ISBN: 0-8010-6128-8.

Mellowes, M. (Producer & Writer). (1998). <u>From Jesus to Christ, The First Christians: Part I.</u> [Motion Picture]. United States: Frontline Producers. ISBN: 0-7806-2288-X.

Mellowes, M. (Producer & Writer). (1998). <u>From Jesus to Christ, The First Christians: Part II.</u> [Motion Picture]. United States: Frontline Producers. ISBN: 0-7806-2288-X.

Mellowes, M. (Producer & Writer). (1998). <u>From Jesus to Christ, The First Christians: Part III.</u> [Motion Picture]. United States: Frontline Producers. ISBN: 0-7806-2288-X.

Mellowes, M. (Producer & Writer). (1998). <u>From Jesus to Christ, The First Christians: Part IV.</u> [Motion Picture]. United States: Frontline Producers. ISBN: 0-7806-2288-X.

Melville, H. (1971). <u>Moby-Dick or The Whale</u> (Collectors ed.). Norwalk, CT: The Easton Press.

Melville, H. (1964). <u>Moby-Dick or, The Whale.</u> New York: Macmillan Publishing Company.

Melville, H. (1967). <u>Moby-Dick or the Whale.</u> New York, NY: Bantam Books, Inc. ISBN: 0-553-21007-6.

Melville, H. (Based on the novel by), Halmi, R., Coppola, F.F., & Fuchs, F. (Executive Producers) (1998). <u>Moby Dick.</u> [Motion Picture]. United States: Whale Productions Limited. ISBN: 1-57192-530-X.

Merchant, C. (1989). Ecological Revolutions: Nature, Gender, and Science in New England. Chapel Hill, NC: The University of North Carolina Press. ISBN: 0-8078-4254-0.
Mergen, B. (2000). Globalization, Transnationalism, and the End of the American Century: Can American Studies be Globalized? *American Studies.* Summer/Fall 2000. 41:2/3. Pp. 303-320.
Merriam-Webster Inc., & Gove, P. (Ed. in Chief). (1986). Webster's Third New International Dictionary of the English Language: Unabridged. Springfield, MA: Merriam-Webster Inc. ISBN: 0-87779-201-1.
Merriam-Webster Inc., & Woolf, H.B. (Ed. in Chief). (1974). The Merriam-Webster Dictionary. Springfield, MA: Merriam-Webster Inc. ISBN: 0-671-52612.
Meyers, D. (1992). Psychology (3rd ed.). New York: Worth Publishers. ISBN: 0-87901-506-3.
Michaud, S., & Aynesworth, H. (1989). Ted Bundy: Conversations with a Killer. New York: Signet. ISBN: 0-451-16355-9.
Michener, J. (1980). The Covenant. New York: Random House.
Michener, J. (1985). Texas. New York: Ballantine Books. ISBN: 0-449-21092-8.
Michener, J. (1988). Alaska. New York: Fawcett Crest. ISBN: 0-449-21726-4.
Michener, J. (1992). Mexico. New York: Ballantine Books. ISBN: 0-449-22187-3.
Microsoft. (1998). Microsoft 1998 Annual Report. Redmond, WA: Microsoft Corporation.
Mill, J. (1994). Principles of Political Economy. Oxford: Oxford University Press. ISBN: -19-283672-2.
Mill, J., with an introduction by Dershowitz, A. (1993). On Liberty and Utilitarianism. New York: Bantam Books. ISBN: 0-553-21414-4.
Miller, F. (1942). General Douglas MacArthur; Fighter for Freedom: An Authentic Life Story. Chicago, IL: The John C. Winston Company.
Miller, G. (1998). The Prentice Hall Reader (5th ed.). Upper Saddle River, NJ: Prentice Hall. ISBN: 0-13-645599-9.
Miller, N. (1992). Theodore Roosevelt: A Life. New York: William Morrow and Company. ISBN: 0-688-13220-0.
Miller, R. (1991). Running a Meeting That Works. New York: Barron's Educational Series, Inc. ISBN: 0-8120-4640-4.
Miller, R. (Ed.). (1992). The Complete Gospels. Sonoma, CA: Polebridge Press. ISBN: 0-06-065587-9.
Miller, T. (1981). State Government in Wyoming. Dubuque, IA: Kendall/Hunt Publishing Company. ISBN: 0-843-2362-X.
Millman, J. (1979). Micro-Electronics: Digital and Analog Circuits and Systems. New York: McGraw-Hill Book Company. ISBN: 0-07-042327-X.

Milton, J. (1968). Paradise Lost and Paradise Regained. Ricks, C. (Ed.). New York: A Signet Classic. Library of Congress Catalog Card Number: 68-17059.

Mintz, S.W. (1996). Tasting Food, Tasting Freedom: Excursions into Eating, Culture, and the Past. Boston, MA. Beacon Press. ISBN: 0-8070-4629-9.

Mirowski, P. (Ed.). (1994). Edgeworth on Chance, Economic Hazard, and Statistics. Lanham, MD: Rowman & Littlefield Publishers, Inc. ISBN: 0-8476-7751-6.

Mishkin, F. (1998). The Economics of Money, Banking, and Financial Markets (5th ed.). Reading, MA: Addison-Wesley Longman, Inc. ISBN: 0-321-01440-5.

Mishkin, F., & Eakins, S. (1998). Financial Markets and Institutions (2nd ed.). Reading, MA: Addison-Wesley. ISBN: 0-321-01465-0.

Mitchell, William J. (1996). *City of Bits: Space, Place, and the Infobahn.* U.S.A. [On-line]. Available: http://mitpress.mit.edu/e-books/**City_of_Bits**.

Mix, D., & Schmitt, N. (1985). Circuit Analysis for Engineers: Continuous and Discrete Time Systems. New York: John Wiley & Sons. ISBN: 0-471-08432-8.

Montagu, A. (1970). The Direction of Human Development (Rev. ed.). New York: Hawthorn Books, Inc. Library of Congress Catalog Card Number: 72-107636.

Montana, P., & Charnov, B. (1993). Management (2nd ed.). New York: Barron's Educational Series. ISBN: 0-8120-1549-5.

Moore, M. (1996). Downsize This! Random Threats from an Unarmed American. New York: Crown Publishers, Inc. ISBN: 0-517-70739-X.

Moore, M. (Speaker) (1996). Downsize This: Random Threats from an Unarmed American. (Cassette Recording). New York: Random House. ISBN: 0-679-45806-9.

Morgan, WM. Capt. (1827). Illustrations of Masonry. New York: Col. David C. Miller.[Returned to Uncle Ralph May 7, 2002]

Morita, A., & Ishihara, S. (1990). The Japan That Can Say "No". Washington, D.C.: The Jefferson Educational Foundation.

Morris, E. (1999). Dutch: A Memoir of Ronald Reagan. New York: Random House. ISBN: 0-394-55508-2.

Morris, K., & Siegel, A. (1992). Guide to Understanding Personal Finance. New York: Lightbulb Press, Inc. ISBN: 0-671-87964-2.

Morris, W. & M., with foreword by Asimov, I. (1988). Morris Dictionary of Work and Phrase Origins (2nd ed.). New York: Harper & Row Publishers. ISBN: 0-06-015862-X.

Morris-Suzuki, T. (1984). Showa: An Inside History of Hirohito's Japan. New York: Schocken Books. ISBN: 0-8052-3944-8.

Morse-Cluley, E., & Read, R. (Speakers) (1989). Webster's New World Power Vocabulary-Volume 1. (Cassette Recording). New York: Simon & Schuster. ISBN: 0-671-68899-5.

Motley, W. (1947). Knock on any Door. New York: D. Appleton-Century Company, Inc.

Moulin, H. (1995). Cooperative Microeconomics: A Game-Theoretic Introduction. Princeton, NJ: Princeton University Press. ISBN: 0-691-03481-8.

Moursund, D. (1998). Is Information Technology Improving Education? *Learning and Leading with Technology*. Vol. 26. Number 4. December/January 1998-99. Pp. 4-5.

Mowat, F. (1973). Never Cry Wolf. New York: Bantam Books. ISBN: 0-553-27396-5.

Mullish, H. (1976). A Basic Approach to Basic. New York: John Wiley & Sons. ISBN: 0-471-62375-X.

Murphy, W., & Pritchett, C.H. (1979). Courts, Judges, and Politics: An Introduction to the Judicial Process (3rd ed.). New York: Random House. ISBN: 0-394-32117-0.

Murray, A.L., & Wiles, E. (1925). A First Book in English for High Schools (Rev. ed.). Boston, MA: D.C. Heath and Company.

Myers, P., & Solomon, P. (1994). Registered Representative Stockbroker NASD Series 7 Exam. New York, NY: ARCO. ISBN: 0-671-88314-3.

Nabhan, G.P. (1997). Cultures of Habitat: On Nature, Culture, and Story. Washington, D.C.: Counterpoint. ISBN: 1-887178-96-1.

Naisbitt, J. (1982). Megatrends: Ten New Directions Transforming our Lives. New York, NY: Warner Books Inc. ISBN: 0-446-90991-2.

Naisbitt, J. (1994). Global Paradox: The Bigger the World Economy, the More Powerful its Smallest Players. New York, NY: William Morrow and Company, Inc. ISBN: 0-688-12791-6.

Naisbitt, J. (1996). Megatrends Asia: Eight Asian Megatrends that are Reshaping our World. New York, NY: Simon & Schuster. ISBN: 0-684-81542-7.

Naisbitt, J. (1999). High Tech High Touch: Technology and our Search for Meaning. New York, NY: Broadway Books. ISBN: 0-7679-0383-8.

Naisbitt, J., & Aburdene, P. (1985). Reinventing the Corporation. New York: Warner Books. ISBN: 0-446-51284-2.

Naisbitt, J., & Aburdene, P. (1990). Megatrends 2000: Ten New Directions for the 1990's. New York, NY: Avon Books. ISBN: 0-380-70437-4.

National Bureau of Economic Research. (1956). Policies to Combat Depression. Princeton, NJ: Princeton University Press. Library of Congress Catalog Card Number: 55-10681.

National Collegiate Athletic Association. (1999). 2000 Official Rules of Basketball. Chicago, IL: Triumph Books.

Nebergall, W., Holtzclaw, H. Jr., & Robinson W. (1980). General Chemistry (6th ed.). Lexington, MA: D.C. Heath and Company. ISBN: 0-669-2218-7.

Negroponte, N. (1995). Being Digital. New York, NY: Alfred A. Knopf. Inc. UW Science Libr Call #: TK 5103.7.N43 1995. 0-679-43919-6.

Nelson, A., Folley, K., & Borgman (1946). Calculus (Rev. ed.). Boston, MA: D.C. Heath and Company.

Neuharth, A. (Speaker) (1990). Confessions of an S.O.B. (Cassette Recording). New York: Bantam Audio Publishing. ISBN: 0-553-45242-8.

Neumann, J., & Morgenstern, O. (1972). Theory of Games and Economic Behavior. Princeton, NJ: Princeton University Press. ISBN: 0-691-00362-9.

Neusner, J. (1977). The Tosefta: Sixth Division TOHOROT The Order of the Purities. New York: KTAV Publishing House Inc.

Neustadt, K. (1992). Clambake: A History & Celebration of an American Tradition. Amherst: The University of Massachusetts Press.

Nevins, A., & Commager, H. (1956). A Short History of The United States. New York: The Modern Library. Library of Congress Catalog Card Number: 57-14926.

Nichols, E., Anderson, P., Dwight, L., Flournoy, F., Kalin, R., Schluep, J., & Simon, L. (1978). High School Mathematics. New York: Holt, Rinehart and Winston. ISBN: 0-03-018571-8.

Nickerson, W. (1969). How I Turned $1,000 into Three Million in Real Estate-In My Spare Time (Rev. ed.). New York: Simon & Schuster. ISBN: 0-671-20125-5.

Nierenberg, G. (1968). The Art of Negotiating. New York: Barnes & Noble Books. ISBN: 1-56619-816-X.

Nixon, R. (1992). Seize the Moment: America's Challenge in a One-Superpower World. New York: Simon & Schuster. ISBN: 0-671-74343-0.

Nixon, R. (Speaker) (1990). In the Arena. (Cassette Recording). New York: Simon & Schuster.

Noble, David F. (1998). Digital Diploma Mills, Part I: The Automation of Higher Education. *October*. Vol. 86. Fall 1998. Pp107-117.

Nolan, Christopher. (1987). Under the Eye of the Clock: The Life Story of Christopher Nolan. New York, NY: St. Martin's Press. ISBN: 0-312-01266-7

Norris, R., Harries, K. & Vitek, J. (1982). Geography: An Introductory Perspective. Columbus, OH: Charles E. Merrill Publishing Company. ISBN: 0-675-09885-8.

O'Neill, S.T., with Gary Hymel. (1994). All Politics is Local: and Other Rules of the Game. New York, NY: Times Books. ISBN: 0-8129-2297-2.

O'Neill, S.T., with William Novak. (1987). Man of the House: The Life and Political Memoirs of Speaker Tip O'Neill. New York, NY: Random House. ISBN: 0-394-55201-6.

Office of the Federal Register; National Archives and Records Administration. (1989). The United States Government Manual 1989/90 (Rev. ed.). Washington, D.C.: U.S. Government Printing Office.

Olasky, M., with preface by Murray, C. (1992). The Tragedy of American Compassion. Washington, D.C.: Regenery Publishing Inc. ISBN: 0-89526-725-X.

Olmos, E., Ybarra, L., & Monterrey, M. (1999). Americanos: Latino Life in the United States. Boston, MA: Little, Brown and Company. ISBN: 0-316-64909-0.

Orwell, G. (1945). Animal Farm. Penguin Audio Books. ISBN: 0-14-086251-X.

Osborne, T. (1999). Faith in the Game: Lessons on Football, Work, and Life. Colorado Springs, CO: WaterBrook Press. ISBN: 0-7679-0422-2.

Ostrovsky, V., & Hoy, C. (1990). By Way of Deception. New York: St. Martin's Paperbacks. ISBN: 0-312-92614-6.

Oursler, F. (1949). The Greatest Story Ever Told. Garden City, NY: Permabooks.

Oxford University Press. (1979). The Oxford Dictionary of Quotations (3rd ed.). New York: Oxford University Press.

Packer, B., with Lazenby, R. (1985). HOOPS! Confessions of a College Basketball Analyst. Chicago, IL: Contemporary Books, Inc. ISBN: 0-8092-5305-4.

Packer, B., with Lazenby, R. (1989). Golden Moments of the Final Four. Dallas, TX: Jefferson Street Press, Taylor Publishing Co.

Page, M. (Writer), Yeager, T. & Ellis, L. (Producers). (2000). The Next Big Thing? [Motion Picture]. United States: Kikim Media and Quest Productions.

Pagels, E. (1979). The Gnostic Gospels. New York: Vintage Books. ISBN: 0-679-72453-2.

Paine, T. (1969). Common Sense, The Rights of Man, and Other Essential Writings of Thomas Paine. New York: Meridian. Library of Congress Catalog Card Number: 84-60856.

Parkin, M. (1994). Macroeconomics (Updated 2nd ed.). Reading, MA: Addison-Wesley Publishing Company. ISBN: 0-201-50033-7.

Parkin, M. (1994). Macroeconomics (Updated 2nd ed.). Reading, MA: Addison-Wesley Publishing Company. ISBN: 0-201-50032-9.

Parrillo, D.F. (1992). The NASDAQ Handbook: The Stock Market for the Next 100 Years. Chicago, IL: Probus Publishing Company. ISBN: 1-55738-403-7.

Pasachoff, J. (1983). Astronomy: From the Earth to the Universe (2nd ed.). Philadelphia, PA: Saunders College Publishing. ISBN: 0-03-058419-1.

Patterson, C.H. (1963). Cliffs Notes on Plato's The Republic. Lincoln, NE: Cliffs Notes Inc. ISBN: 0-8220-1129-8.

Paulos, J.A. (1988). Innumeracy: Mathematical Illiteracy and Its Consequences. New York, NY: Hill and Wang. ISBN: 0-8090-7447-8.

Paulos, J.A. (1991). Beyond Numeracy: Ruminations of a Numbers Man. New York: Alfred A. Knopf. ISBN: 0-394-58640-9.

Payson, P. (Producer). (1995). Great American Speeches: 80 Years of Political Oratory. [Motion Picture]. United States: Pieri & Spring Productions. ISBN: 0-9649168-0-0.

Pearson, R. (1990). Probable Cause. New York: St. Martin's Paperbacks. ISBN: 0-312-92385-6.

Peisch, J. (Producer), & Walworth, A. (Executive Producer). (1999). Yogi Berra: Deja Vu All Over Again. [Motion Picture]. United States: New River Media. (Available at www.nrmedia.com)

Penney, E. (1991). The Facts on File Dictionary of Film and Broadcast Terms. New York: Facts on File. ISBN: 0-8160-2782-X.

Perot, R. (1992). United We Stand: How We can Take Back Our Country: A Plan for the 21st Century. New York. NY: Hyperion. ISBN: 1-56282-852-5.

Perrin, D. (2000). American Fan: Sports Mania and the Culture that Feeds it. New York: Avon Books Inc.

Peter, L. (1977). Peter's Quotations: Ideas for Our Time. New York: Bantam Books. ISBN: 0-553-27140-7.

Peters, T. (Speaker) (1987). Thriving on Chaos. (Cassette Recording). New York: Random House. ISBN: 0-394-56099-X.

Peters, T., & Austin, N. (1985). A Passion for Excellence: The Leadership Difference. New York: Warner Books. ISBN: 0-446-38348-1.

Peters, T., & Waterman, R., Jr. (1982). In Search of Excellence. New York: Warner Books. ISBN: 0-446-38389-9.

Peterson, L., Brereton, J., & Hartman, J. (1996). A Guide to The Norton Reader (9th ed.). New York: W.W. Norton & Company. ISBN: 0-393-96828-6.

Philbrick, N. (2000). In the Heart of the Sea: The Tragedy of the Whaleship Essex. New York: The Penguin Group. ISBN: 0-670-89157-6.

Pillsbury, R. (1998). No Foreign Food: The American Diet in Time and Place. Boulder, CO: Westview Press. ISBN: 0-8133-2739-3.

Pindyck, R., & Rubinfeld, D. (1995). Macroeconomics (3rd ed.). Englewood Cliffs, NJ: Prentice Hall. ISBN: 0-02-395900-2.

Pitcher, G. (2001). McFadden: The Town They Called "Camp". Unk: Goldie Norah Pitcher.

Plater, Z., Abrams, R., & Goldfarb, W. (1992). Environmental Law and Policy: A Coursebook on Nature, Law, and Society. St. Paul, MN: West Publishing Company. ISBN: 0-314-00341-X.
Plato. (1954). The Last Days of Socrates. London, England: Penguin Classics. ISBN: 0-14-044037-2.
Plato. (1987). The Republic. Eds. Betty Radice. London, England. Penguin Books. 0-14-044048-8.
Plotnik, A. (1982). The Elements of Editing: A Modern Guide for Editors and Journalists. New York: MacMillan Publishing Co., Inc. ISBN: 0-02-04741-5.
Pool, R. (1997). Beyond Engineering: How Society Shapes Technology. Oxford, NY: Oxford U. Press. ISBN: 0-19-512911-3.
Popcorn, F. (Speaker) (1991). The Popcorn Report. (Cassette Recording). New York: Simon & Schuster. ISBN: 0-671-74942-0.
Popenoe, D. (1974). Sociology (2nd ed.). Englewood Cliffs, NJ: Prentice-Hall, Inc. ISBN: 0-13-821827-7.
Poundstone, W. (1992). Prisoner's Dilemma. New York: Doubleday. ISBN: 0-385-41580-X.
Pournelle, J. (Ed.). (1979). The Endless Frontier, Vol. 1. New York: Ace Science Fiction Books. ISBN: 0-441-20669-7.
Powell, C., with Persico, J. (1995, 1996). My American Journey. New York: Ballantine Books. ISBN: 0-345-40728-8.
Preston, R. (1991). American Steel: Hot Metal Men and the Resurrection of the Rust Belt. New York: Prentice Hall Press. ISBN: 0-13-029604-X.
Propp, V. (1968). Morphology of the Folktale. Austin: University of Texas Press. Coe Ref #: GR 550.P7613 1968.
Prosser, F., & Winkel, M. (1981). Computer Organization. USA: Professor Publishing.
Public Broadcasting System. (1999). The 50 Years War: Israel and the Arabs. [Motion Picture]. United States: Brian Lapping Associates and WGBH Educational Foundation. ISBN: 0-7806-2593-5.
Pursell, C. (1995). The Machine in America: A Social History of Technology. Baltimore, MD.
Putnam, R.D. (2000). Bowling Alone: The Collapse and Revival of American Community. New York, NY: ISBN: 0-684-83283-6.
Quinn, G., & Allan, C. (Producers). (1995). Hoop Dreams. [Motion Picture]. United States: Turner Home Entertainment. ISBN: 0-7806-0565-9.
Radcliffe, R. (1997). Investment Concepts: Analysis: Strategy (5th ed.). Reading, MA: Addison-Wesley. ISBN: 0-673-99988-2.
Rader, M. (Ed.). (1980). The Enduring Questions: Main Problems of Philosophy (4th ed.). New York: Holt, Rinehart, and Winston. ISBN: 0-03-055406-3.

Radio Shack. (1986). Semiconductor Reference Guide. Fort Worth, TX: Tandy Corporation.

Radway, J.A. (1984). Reading the Romance: Women, Patriarchy, and Popular Literature. Chapel Hill, NC: The University of North Carolina Press. ISBN: 0-8078-4349-0.

Rasmusen, E. (1989). Games and Information: An Introduction to Game Theory (2nd ed.). Cambridge, MA: Blackwell Publishers. ISBN: 1-55786-502-7.

Rawlins, G. (1996). Moths to the Flame. Cambridge, MA: A Bradford Book. ISBN: 0-262-18176-2.

Rawlins, G.J.E. (1996). Moths to the Flame: The Seductions of Computer Technology. U.S.A. MIT Press. ISBN: 0-262-18176-2.

Reagan, R. (1968). The Creative Society. New York: The Devin-Adair Company. Library of Congress Catalog Card Number: 68-26085.

Reagan, R. (1989). Speaking My Mind. (Cassette Recording). New York: Simon & Schuster. ISBN: 0-671-69341-7.

Reagan, R. (1990). An American Life. (Cassette Recording). New York: Simon & Schuster. ISBN: 0-671-72630-7.

Reagan, R. (1999). Ronald Reagan: The Great Communicator: Volume 1: The Reagan Presidency (1981-1989). [Motion Picture]. United States: Hail to the Chief Productions. ISBN: 0-7886-0179-2.

Reagan, R. (1999). Ronald Reagan: The Great Communicator: Volume 2: The Military and the Soviet Union. [Motion Picture]. United States: Hail to the Chief Productions. ISBN: 0-7886-0179-2.

Reagan, R. (1999). Ronald Reagan: The Great Communicator: Volume 3: Reagan on Government and the American Dream. [Motion Picture]. United States: Hail to the Chief Productions. ISBN: 0-7886-0179-2.

Reagan, R. (1999). Ronald Reagan: The Great Communicator: Volume 4: The Man. [Motion Picture]. United States: Hail to the Chief Productions. ISBN: 0-7886-0179-2.

Reagan, Ronald. (1990). An American Life. New York, NY: Simon and Schuster. ISBN: 0-671-69198-8.

Rees, E.R. (1991). The Iliad of Homer. New York, NY: Oxford University Press. ISBN: 0-19-506826-2.

Reichman, R. (1992). Formatting Your Screenplay. New York: Paragon House. ISBN: 1-55778-434-5.

Reilly, F. (1986). Investments (2nd ed.). Chicago, IL: The Dryden Press. ISBN: 0-03-001847-1.

Reilly, F. (1989). Investment Analysis and Portfolio Management (3rd ed.). Chicago, IL: The Dryden Press. ISBN: 0-03-025498-1.

Reimer, K. (1994). 1001 Ways to Help Your Child Walk With God. Wheaton, IL: Tyndale House Publishers, Inc. ISBN: 0-8423-4605-8.

Reisner, M. (1986). Cadillac Desert: The American West and Its Disappearing Water. New York, NY: Penguin Books. ISBN: 0-14-017824-4.

Restak, R.M. (1988). The Mind: The Official Companion Volume to the Landmark PBS Television Series. New York, NY: Bantam Books. ISBN: 0-553-05314-0.

Rhodes, F. (1991). Geology. Racine, WI: Western Publishing Company. ISBN: 0-307-24349-4.

Ricardo, D. (1996). Principles of Political Economy and Taxation. New York: Prometheus Books. ISBN: 1-57392-109-2.

Rice, J. (1971). Lodges Examined by the Bible. Murfreesboro, TN: Sword of the Lord. ISBN: 0-87398-510-9.

Ridenour, F. (1967). So What's the Difference? Glendale, CA: Regal Books. ISBN: 0-8307-0001-3.

Ringer, R.J. (1974). Winning Through Intimidation. New York, NY: Fawcett Crest Book. ISBN: 0-449-20786-2.

Ripley, R. (1934). Ripley's Believe It Or Not. Garden City, NY: Garden City Publishing Company.

Riso, D., & Hudson, R. (1996). Personality Types: Using the Enneagram for Self-Discovery (Rev. ed.). New York: Houghton Mifflin Company. ISBN: 0-395-79864-I.

Ritvo, H. (1987). The Animal Estate: The English and Other Creatures in the Victorian Age. Cambridge: Harvard University Press. UW Sci Library Reference Number: SF53.R58 1987

Roberts, P. (Ed.). (1982). More Buffalo Bones. Wyoming: Wyoming State Archives, Museums, and Historical Department. ISBN: 0-943398-00-2.

Roberts, R. (1994). The Choice: A Fable of Free Trade and Protectionism. Upper Saddle River, NJ: Prentice-Hall, Inc. ISBN: 0-13-083008-9.

Robinson, D. (1990). Life on the Edge. U.S.A.: Ranger Rob Distributing Company.

Robinson, P. (1994). Snapshots from Hell: The Making of an MBA. New York, NY: Warner Books. ISBN: 0-446-51786-0.

Rocky Mountain News. (1993). Rocky Mountain News Stock Guide, 1993. New York: McGraw-Hill.

Roe, E.T. (1920). New American Business Cyclopedia. Chicago, IL: Gordon G. Sapp.

Roget, P.M. (1977). Roget's International Thesaurus (4th ed., Rev. by Chapman, R.). New York: Thomas Y. Crowell, Publishers. ISBN: 0-690-00010-3.

Roget, P.M. (1978). <u>Roget's College Thesaurus in Dictionary Form.</u> (Rev. by Morehead, P.). New York: A Signet Book.

Rooney, A. (1986). <u>Word for Word.</u> New York: G.P. Putnam's Sons. ISBN: 0-399-13200-7.

Roosevelt, T. (1998). <u>Hunting Trips of a Ranchman: Sketches of Sport on the Northern Cattle Plains & The Wilderness Hunter: An Account of the Big Game of the United States and its Chase with Horse, Hound, and Rifle.</u> New York: The Modern Library.

Rosmini, A. (1991). <u>Certainty.</u> Durham, U.K.: Rosmini House.

Ross, S., & Westerfield, R. (1988). <u>Corporate Finance.</u> St. Louis, MO: Times Mirror/ Mosby College Publishing. ISBN: 0-8016-4211-6.

Rossiter, C. (Ed.). (1961). <u>The Federalist Papers: Hamilton, Madison, and Jay.</u> New York: The Penguin Group. Library of Congress Catalog Card Number: 61-10757.

Rosten, L. (1996). <u>The Joys of Yiddish.</u> New York, NY: Pocket Books. ISBN: 0-7434-0651-6.

Rowe, J.C. (2000). <u>Globalism and the New American Studies</u>. Ed. by John Carlos Rowe. *Post-Nationalist American Studies.* Los Angeles, CA: University of California Press. Pp. 29, 32-33.

Rukeyser, L. (1983). <u>What's Ahead for the Economy.</u> New York: Simon and Schuster. ISBN: 0-671-44996-6.

Rule, A. (1989). <u>The Stranger Beside Me: Ted Bundy</u> (Rev. ed.). New York: Signet. ISBN: 0-451-16493-8.

Rush, M. (1998). <u>Instructor's Manual: Parkin Economics</u> (4th ed.). Reading, MA: Addison-Wesley. ISBN: 0-201-32764-3.

Ryan, J., & Durning, A. (1997). <u>Stuff: The Secret Lives of Everyday Things.</u> Seattle, WA: Northwest Environment Watch. ISBN: 1-886093-04-0.

Ryan, J.C. (1997). <u>Stuff: The Secret Lives of Everyday Things</u>. Vancouver, B.C.: Northwest Environmental Watch. ISBN: 1-886093-04-0.

Sackett, S. (1990). <u>Box Office Hits.</u> New York: Billboard Books. ISBN: 0-8230-7549-4.

Safire, W. (1987). <u>Freedom.</u> Garden City, NY: Doubleday & Company, Inc. ISBN: 0-385-15903-X.

Sagan, C. (1980). <u>Cosmos.</u> New York: Ballantine Books. ISBN: 0-345-33135-4.

Sagan, C. (1985). <u>Contact</u>. New York, NY: Pocket Books. ISBN: 0-671-43422-5.

Saint Augustine. (1961). <u>Confessions.</u> London: The Penguin Group.

Sale, R. (1970). <u>On Writing.</u> New York: Random House. Library of Congress Catalog Card Number: 73-90939.

Salisbury, H. (Introduction) (1964). Report of the Warren Commission on the Assassination of President Kennedy. New York: McGraw-Hill Book Company. Library of Congress Catalog Card Number: 64-24803.
Salmon, M. (1995). Introduction to Logic and Critical Thinking (3rd ed.). Orlando, FL: Harcourt Brace. ISBN: 0-15-543064-5.
Samuelson, L. (1997). Evolutionary Games and Equilibrium Selection. Cambridge, MA: The MIT Press. ISBN: 0-262-69219-8.
Samuelson, P. (1947). Foundations of Economic Analysis. Cambridge, MA: Harvard University Press. ISBN: 0-674-3131-1.
Samuelson, P., & Nordhaus, W. (1998). Economics (16th ed.). Boston, MA: Irwin McGraw-Hill. ISBN: 0-07-115542-2.
Sandeen, E.J. (1995). Picturing an Exhibition: The Family of Man and 1950's America. Albuquerque, NM: University of New Mexico Press. ISBN: 0-8263-1558-5.
Santrock, J. (1988). Psychology: The Science of Mind and Behavior (2nd ed.). Dubuque, IA: Wm. C. Brown Publishers. ISBN: 0-697-06725-4.
Sarason, I., & Sarason, B. (1980). Abnormal Psychology (3rd ed.). Englewood Cliffs, NJ: Prentice-Hall, Inc. ISBN: 0-13-001107-X.
Schaeffer, R. (1997). Understanding Globalization: The Social Consequences of Political, Economic, and Environmental Change. Lanham, MD: Rowman & Littlefield Publishers, Inc. ISBN: 0-8476-8651-6.
Schall, L., & Haley, C. (1991). Introduction to Financial Management (6th ed.). New York: McGraw-Hill, Inc. ISBN: 0-07-055117-0.
Schiller, B. (1997). The Economy Today (7th ed.). New York: The McGraw-Hill Companies, Inc. ISBN: 0-07-057711-0.
Schiller, B. (1997). The Macro Economy Today (7th ed.). New York: The McGraw-Hill Companies, Inc. ISBN: 0-07-057715-3.
Schlomith, Rimmon-Kenan (1983). Narrative Fiction. New York: Methuen.
Schmitt, P.J. (1990). Back to Nature: The Arcadian Myth in Urban America. Baltimore, MD: The Johns Hopkins University Press. ISBN: 0-8018-4013-9.
Schnoebelen, W., & Spencer, J. (1987). Mormonism's Temple of Doom. Boise, ID: Triple J Publishers.
Schnoebelen, W., & Spencer, J. (1990). Whited Sepulchers. Boise, ID: Triple J Publishers.
Schonberger, R., & Knod, E. Jr. (1994). Operations Management: Continuous Improvement (5th ed.). Burr Ridge, IL: Irwin. ISBN: 0-256-11218-5.
Schrager, S. (1999). The Trial Lawyer's Art. Philadelphia: Temple University Press.
Schullery, P. (1988). The Bear Hunter's Century. New York: Dodd & Mead.
Schumpeter, J. (1951). Ten Great Economists: From Marx to Keynes. New York: Oxford University Press.

Schumpeter, J., with an introduction by Bottomore, T. (1942). <u>Capitalism, Socialism, and Democracy</u> (3rd ed.). New York: HarperPerennial. ISBN: 0-06-133008-6.

Schwartz, A. (1992). <u>Delegating Authority.</u> New York: Barron's Educational Series, Inc. ISBN: 0-8120-4958-6.

Schwartz, J. (1959). <u>The Magic of Thinking Big.</u> North Hollywood, CA: Wilshire Book Company. ISBN: 0-87980-092-5.

Scofield, C.I. (Ed.). (1937). <u>The Holy Bible.</u> New York: Oxford University Press.

Scott, D., Martin, J., Petty, J.W., Keown, A., Thatcher, J., & Graham, S. (1993). <u>Cases in Finance</u> (3rd ed.). Englewood Cliffs, NJ: Prentice-Hall, Inc. ISBN: 0-13-117995-0.

Scourby, A. (Narrator). <u>The New Testament</u> (Cassette Recording, Tape 1). Tampa, FL: Neva Products, Inc.

Scourby, A. (Narrator). <u>The New Testament</u> (Cassette Recording, Tape 2). Tampa, FL: Neva Products, Inc.

Scourby, A. (Narrator). <u>The New Testament</u> (Cassette Recording, Tape 3). Tampa, FL: Neva Products, Inc.

Scourby, A. (Narrator). <u>The New Testament</u> (Cassette Recording, Tape 4). Tampa, FL: Neva Products, Inc.

Scourby, A. (Narrator). <u>The New Testament</u> (Cassette Recording, Tape 5). Tampa, FL: Neva Products, Inc.

Scourby, A. (Narrator). <u>The New Testament</u> (Cassette Recording, Tape 6). Tampa, FL: Neva Products, Inc.

Scourby, A. (Narrator). <u>The New Testament</u> (Cassette Recording, Tape 7). Tampa, FL: Neva Products, Inc.

Scourby, A. (Narrator). <u>The New Testament</u> (Cassette Recording, Tape 8). Tampa, FL: Neva Products, Inc.

Scourby, A. (Narrator). <u>The New Testament</u> (Cassette Recording, Tape 9). Tampa, FL: Neva Products, Inc.

Scourby, A. (Narrator). <u>The New Testament</u> (Cassette Recording, Tape 10). Tampa, FL: Neva Products, Inc.

Scourby, A. (Narrator). <u>The New Testament</u> (Cassette Recording, Tape 11). Tampa, FL: Neva Products, Inc.

Scourby, A. (Narrator). <u>The New Testament</u> (Cassette Recording, Tape 12). Tampa, FL: Neva Products, Inc.

Scoville, C.R., & Towner, D.B., (Ed.) (Unknown). <u>The King of Glory.</u> Chicago, IL: The Charles Reign Scoville Publishing Company.

Shaara, J. (1996). <u>Gods and Generals.</u> New York: Ballantine Books. ISBN: 0-345-40957-4.

Shaara, J. (1998). *The Last Full Measure.* New York: Ballantine Books. ISBN: 0-345-42548-0.

Shaara, M. (1974). *The Killer Angels.* New York: Ballantine Books. ISBN: 0-345-34810-9.

Shanahan, M., with Schefter, A. (1999). *Think Like a Champion: Building Success One Victory as a Time.* New York, NY: HarperBusiness. ISBN: 0-06-662039-2.

Shapiro, C., & Varian, H. (1999). *Information Rules: A Strategic Guide to the Network Economy.* Boston, MA: Harvard Business School Press. ISBN: 0-87584-863-X.

Shapo, H., Shapo, M. (1996). *Law School Without Fear: Strategies for Success.* Westbury, New York: The Foundation Press.

Sharpe, W., Alexander, G., & Bailey, J. (1995). *Investments* (5th ed.). Englewood Cliffs, NJ: Prentice-Hall, Inc. ISBN: 0-13-103771-4.

Sharpe, W., Alexander, G., & Baily, J. (1999). *Investments* (6th ed.). Upper Saddle River, NJ: Prentice-Hall, Inc. ISBN: 0-13-010130-3.

Shaughnessy, J. (1996). *Texas Gold: "Growing up in a Texas oil camp".* Alvin, TX: Swan Publishing. ISBN: 0-943629-24-1.

Shea, E. (1993). *Antidote for Cabin Fever.* Bessemer, AL: Colonial Press. ISBN: 1-56883035-1.

Sherry, S., Drew, C., & Drew, A.L. (1998). *Blind Man's Bluff: The Untold Story of American Submarine Espionage.* New York, NY: Public Affairs Perseus Books Group. ISBN: 1-891620-08-8.

Shertzer, M. (1986). *The Elements of Grammar.* New York: MacMillan Publishing Co., Inc. ISBN: 0-02-15440-2.

Sheth, J., & Eshghi, A. (1989). *Global Financial Perspectives.* Cincinnati, OH: South-Western Publishing Company. ISBN: 0-538-80047-X.

Shiva, S. (1985). *Computer Design and Architecture.* Boston, MA: Little, Brown and Company. ISBN: 0-316-78714-0.

Shogren, J., foreword by Ruckelshaus, W. (Ed.). (1998). *Private Property and the Endangered Species Act.* Austin, TX: University of Texas Press. ISBN: 0-292-77797-X.

Short, K. (1981). *Microprocessors and Programmed Logic.* Englewood Cliffs, NJ: Prentice-Hall, Inc. ISBN: 0-13-581173-2.

Shultz, R., & Smith, R. (1985). *Introduction to Electric Power Engineering.* New York: Harper & Row, Publishers. ISBN: 0-06-046131-4.

Silberberg, E. (1990). *The Structure of Economics: A Mathematical Analysis* (2nd ed.). New York: McGraw-Hill, Inc. ISBN: 0-07-057550-9.

Silberberg, E. (1995). *Principles of Microeconomics.* Englewood Cliffs, New Jersey: Prentice Hall.

Silko, L.M. (1977). Ceremony. New York, NY: Penguin Books. ISBN: 0-14-008683-8.

Silver, H., & Nydahl, J. (1977). Introduction to Engineering Thermodynamics. St. Paul, MN: West Publishing Company. ISBN: 0-8299-0053-5.

Simpson, A.K. (1997). Right in the Old Gazoo: A Lifetime of Scrapping with the Press. New York, NY: William Morrow and Company, Inc. ISBN: 0-688-11358-3.

Simpson, J., Weiner, E. (1989). Oxford English Dictionary (OED) (2nd ed.). New York: Clarendon Press. V.5. Coe Ref PE 1625.087 1989.

Simpson, P.K. (1987). The Community of Cattlemen: A Social History of the Cattle Industry in Southeastern Oregon 1869-1912. Moscow, ID: The University of Idaho Press. ISBN: 0-89301-117-7.

Sims, W. (Ed.). (1956). Baptist Hymnal. Nashville, TN: Convention Press. ISBN: 581-185071.

Sinclair, Upton. (1985). The Jungle. New York, NY: Penguin Classics. ISBN:

Slater, R. (1993). The New GE: How Jack Welch Revived an American Institution. Homewood, IL: Richard D. Irwin, Inc. ISBN: 1-55623-670.

Slotkin, R. (1992). Gunfighter Nation: the myth of the frontier in Twentieth Century America. New York: Maxwell Macmillan International.

Smith, A. (2000). The Theory of Moral Sentiments. New York: Prometheus Books. ISBN: 1-57392-800.

Smith, A. (1976). An Inquiry into the Nature and Causes of The Wealth of Nations. Chicago, IL: The University of Chicago Press. ISBN: 0-226-76374-9.

Smith, G., Arnold, D., & Bizzell, B. (1991). Business Strategy and Policy: Cases (3rd ed.). Boston, MA: Houghton Mifflin Company. ISBN: 0-395-56735-1.

Smith, H. (1976). The Russians. New York: Quadrangle/The New York Times Book Company. ISBN: 0-8129-0521-0.

Smith, K. (1991). The Nature of Mathematics (6th ed.). Pacific Grove, CA: Brooks/Cole Publishing Company. ISBN: 0-534-13914-0.

Smith, R., Sarason, I., & Sarason, B. (1982). Psychology: The Frontiers of Behavior (2nd ed.). New York: Harper & Row Publishers. ISBN: 0-06-045729-5.

Smith, R., Sarason, I., & Sarason, B. (1986). Psychology: The Frontiers of Behavior (3rd ed.). New York: Harper & Row, Publishers. ISBN: 0-06-045728-7.

Smith, S.L. (1991). Succeeding Against the Odds: Strategies and Insights from the Learning Disabled. Los Angeles, CA: Jeremy P. Tarcher, Inc. ISBN: 0-87477-674-0.

Snyder, G. (1969). Turtle Island. New York, NY: A New Directions Book. ISBN: 0-8112-0546-0.

Sobel, R. (1968). The Great Bull Market: Wall Street in the 1920's. New York: W.W. Norton & Company, Inc. Library of Congress Catalog Card Number: 68-19795.

Sobel, R. (1980). The Worldly Economists. New York, NY: The Free Press. ISBN: 0-02-929780-X.

Solberg, C. (1976). Oil Power: The Rise and Imminent Fall of an American Empire. New York: A Mentor Book.

Solso, R. (1988). Cognitive Psychology (2nd ed.). Newton, MA: Allyn and Bacon, Inc. ISBN: -205-10581-5.

Soros, G. (1998). The Crisis of Global Capitalism: Open Society Endangered. New York: Public Affairs. ISBN: 1-891620-27-4.

Southern, R.W. (1971). PDP-8 Programming. Ottawa Ont., Canada: Southcroft Publications.

Spence, G. (1983). Of Murder and Madness: A True Story of Insanity and the Law. Garden City, NY: Doubleday & Company, Inc. ISBN: 0-385-18801-3.

Spence, G. (1986). Trial by Fire: The True Story of a Woman's Ordeal at the Hands of the Law. New York, NY: William Morrow and Company, Inc. ISBN: 0-688-06075-7.

Spence, G. (1989). With Justice for None: Destroying an American Myth. New York, NY: Times Books. ISBN: 0-8129-1696-4.

Spence, G. (1993). From Freedom to Slavery: The Rebirth of Tyranny in America. New York, NY: St. Martin's Press. ISBN: 0-312-09467-1.

Spence, G. (1995). How to Argue and Win Every Time. New York, NY: St. Martin's Press. ISBN: 0-312-11827-9.

Spence, G. (1996). The Making of a Country Lawyer: An Autobiography. New York, NY: St. Martin's Press. ISBN: 0-312-14673-6.

Spence, G. (1997). O.J. the Last Word. New York, NY: St. Martin's Press. ISBN: 0-312-18009-8.

Spence, G. (1998). Give me Liberty! Freeing Ourselves in the Twenty-First Century. New York, NY: St. Martin's Press. ISBN: 0-312-19267-3.

Spence, G. (2001). Half-Moon and Empty Stars. New York, NY: Scribner. ISBN: 0-7432-0276-7.

Spence, G. (2001). Seven Simple Steps to Personal Freedom: An Owner's Manual for Life. New York: St. Martin's Press. ISBN: 0-312-28444-6.

Spence, G., & Polk, A. (1982). Gunning for Justice: My Life and Trials. Garden City, NY: Doubleday & Company Inc. ISBN: 0-385-17703-8.

Spencer, J. (1984). Beyond Mormonism: An Elder's Story. Old Tappan, NJ: Chosen Books. ISBN: 0-8007-9076-6.

Spindel, Carol. (2000). *Dancing at Halftime: Sports and the Controversy over American Indian Mascots.* ISBN: 0-8147-8126-8.

Spong, K. (1983). Banking Regulation: Its Purposes, Implementation, and Effects. Kansas City, MO: Federal Reserve Bank of Kansas City.
Stampp, K. (Ed.). (1965). The Causes of The Civil War. Englewood Cliffs, NJ: Prentice-Hall Inc. Library of Congress Catalog Card Number: 65-14083.
Standefur, J., & Bobo, E.R. (Writers). (1998). The Standard Deviants: Calculus, Part 1. [Motion Picture]. United States: Cerebellum Corporation. ISBN: 1-58198-025-6.
Standefur, J., & Bobo, E.R. (Writers). (1998). The Standard Deviants: Calculus, Part 2. [Motion Picture]. United States: Cerebellum Corporation. ISBN: 1-58198-033-7.
Staudohar, P. (2000). Hunting's Best Short Stories. Chicago: Chicago Review Press.
Stechler, A. (Writer & Editor), & Burns, K., et al (Producers) (1981). Ken Burns' America Collection: Brooklyn Bridge. [Motion Picture]. United States: Florentine Films. ISBN: 0-7806-0810-8.
Steinbeck, J. (1965). Of Mice and Men. New York: Penguin Books. ISBN: 0-14-01-7320-X.
Steinbeck, J. (1992). The Grapes of Wrath. New York: Penguin Books. ISBN: 0 14 01.8640 9.
Steinbeck, J. (1998). The Grapes of Wrath. New York, NY: Harper Audio. ISBN: 0-89845-915-X.
Stephens, J. (Ed.). (2000). Guide to American Studies: Resources 2000. Supplement to *American Quarterly* Vol. 52, # 2, June 2000. Baltimore, MD: The Johns Hopkins University Press.
Stern, G.M. (1976). The Buffalo Creek Disaster. New York, NY: Vintage Books. ISBN: 0-394-72343-0.
Stern, J., & Stern, M. (1991). American Gourmet. New York: HarperCollins Publishers. ISBN: 0-06-016710-6.
Stiers, D.O. (Speaker) (1988). The Cardinal of the Kremlin, by Tom Clancy. (Cassette Recording). New York: Simon & Schuster. ISBN: 0-671-66074-8.
Stiglitz, J. (1997). Principles of Microeconomics (2nd ed.). New York: W.W. Norton & Company. ISBN: 0-393-96929-0.
Stiglitz, J. (1997). Principles of Microeconomics (2nd ed.). New York: W.W. Norton & Company. ISBN: 0-393-96929-0.
Stoll, C. (1989). The Cuckoo's Egg: Tracking a Spy through the Maze of Computer Espionage. New York, NY: Doubleday. ISBN: 0-385-24946-2.
Stoll, C. (1995). Silicon Snake Oil: Second Thoughts on the Information Highway. New York, NY: Doubleday.
Stoll, C. (1999). High Tech Heretic: Why Computers don't belong in the Classroom and other Reflections by a Computer Contrarian. New York, NY: Doubleday. [Bound Galley version]

Stone, G. (1996). Constitutional Law. U.S.A.: Aspen Law & Business.ISBN: 0-316-81791-0.
Stone, W., & Bell, J.G. (1977). Prose Style: A Handbook for Writers (3rd ed.). New York: McGraw-Hill Book Company. ISBN: 0-07-061732-5.
Strieber, W. (1987). Communion: A True Story. New York, NY: Beech tree books. William Morrow and Company, Inc. ISBN: 0-688-07086-8.
Strieber, W., & Bell, A. (1999). The Coming Global Superstorm. New York, NY: Simon & Schuster Audio. ISBN: 0-671-04775-2.
Strong, J. (1890). The Exhaustive Concordance of the Bible. New York: The Methodist Book Concern.
Strong, J. (2001). The Strongest Strong's: Exhaustive Concordance of the Bible. Grand Rapids, MI: Zondervan.
Strunk, W., & White, E.B. (1979). The Elements of Style (3rd ed.). New York: MacMillan Publishing Co., Inc. ISBN: 0-02-418200-1.
Studebaker, J.W., Findley, W.C., Knight, F.B., & Ruch, G.M. (1947). Study Arithmetics. Chicago, IL: Scott, Foresman, and Company.
Studenmund, A.H. (1992). Using Econometrics: A Practical Guide (2nd ed.). New York: HarperCollins Publishers. ISBN: 0-673-52125-7.
Summerville, Jennifer. (2000). Book Review of: Teaching and Learning at a Distance: Foundations of Distance Education by Michael Simonson. *Educational Technology Research and Development*. Vol. 48. Number 2. Pp. 97-8. A quarterly publication of the Association for Educational Communications and Technology. NJ.
Sun Microsystems. (1998). Sun Microsystems, Inc. 1998 Annual Report. Palo Alto, CA: Sun Microsystems, Inc.
Sundstrom, C., Hepworth, W., & Diem, K. (1973). Abundance, Distribution, and Food Habits of the Pronghorn. Cheyenne, WY: Wyoming Game and Fish Department.
Suriano, G. (Ed.). (1993). Great American Speeches. Avenel, NJ: Gramercy Books. ISBN: 0-517-09117-8.
Tamarkin, B. (1993). The MERC: The Emergence of a Global Financial Powerhouse. New York, NY: HarperBusiness. ISBN: 0-88730-516-4.
Tarbell, I.M. (1966). The History of the Standard Oil Company. New York, NY: W.W. Norton & Company. ISBN: 0-393-00496-1.
Taylor, B. (Ed.) (1997). Professional Military Education: An Asset for Peace and Progress. Washington, D.C.: The Center for Strategic and International Studies. ISBN: 0-89206-297-5.
Technical Information Center. (1976). M6800 Programming Reference Manual. Phoenix, AZ: Motorola Inc.

Technical Information Center. (1981). 8-Bit Microprocessor & Peripheral Data. Phoenix, AZ: Motorola Inc.

Technical Information Center. (1985). Motorola Fast and LS TTL Data. Phoenix, AZ: Motorola Inc.

Technical Information Center. (1985). Motorola Schottky TTL Data. Phoenix, AZ: Motorola Inc.

Tellushkin, J. (1992). Jewish Humor: What the Best Jewish Jokes Say about the Jews. New York, NY: William Morrow. ISBN: 0-688-16351-3.

Tessitore, J., & Woolfson, S. (Eds.). (1997). A Global Agenda: Issues Before the 52nd General Assembly of the United Nations. Lanham, MD: Rowman & Littlefield Publishers, Inc. ISBN: 0-8476-8704-X.

Tessla, N., & Childress, D.H. (1993). The Fantastic Inventions of Nikola Tesla. Kempton, IL: Adventures Unlimited Press. ISBN: 0-932813-19-4.

Teweles, R., & Jones, F. (1987). The Futures Game: Who wins, Who Loses, Why? (2nd ed.). New York: McGraw-Hill Book Company. ISBN: 0-07-063734-2.

The Alaska Almanac. (1992). Facts about Alaska (16th ed.). Bothell, WA: Alaska Northwest Books. ISBN: 0-88240-249-8.

The Book of Mormon. (1981). Salt Lake City, UT: The Church of Jesus Christ of Latter-day Saints.

The Cato Institute. (Fall 1997). An Interdisciplinary Journal Of Public Policy Analysis. The Cato Journal, Vol. 17(#2), ISSN:0273-3072.

The College Board. (1994). The College Handbook: 1995 (32nd ed.). New York: College Entrance Examination Board. ISBN: 0-87447-490-6.

The Columbia House Company. (1992). Spies: Aerial Reconnaissance. [Motion Picture]. (Available from: Columbia House Video Library, 1400 North Fruitage Avenue, Terre Haute, IN, 47811)

The Columbia House Company. (1992). Spies: Assassination. [Motion Picture]. (Available from: Columbia House Video Library, 1400 North Fruitage Avenue, Terre Haute, IN, 47811)

The Columbia House Company. (1992). Spies: Atomic Bomb Espionage. [Motion Picture]. (Available from: Columbia House Video Library, 1400 North Fruitage Avenue, Terre Haute, IN, 47811)

The Columbia House Company. (1992). Spies: CIA Operations. [Motion Picture]. (Available from: Columbia House Video Library, 1400 North Fruitage Avenue, Terre Haute, IN, 47811)

The Columbia House Company. (1992). Spies: Code Breaking. [Motion Picture]. (Available from: Columbia House Video Library, 1400 North Fruitage Avenue, Terre Haute, IN, 47811)

The Columbia House Company. (1992). Spies: FBI Counterintelligence. [Motion Picture]. (Available from: Columbia House Video Library, 1400 North Fruitage Avenue, Terre Haute, IN, 47811)

The Columbia House Company. (1992). Spies: Mishandling Intelligence. [Motion Picture]. (Available from: Columbia House Video Library, 1400 North Fruitage Avenue, Terre Haute, IN, 47811)

The Columbia House Company. (1992). Spies: Sexpionage. [Motion Picture]. (Available from: Columbia House Video Library, 1400 North Fruitage Avenue, Terre Haute, IN, 47811)

The Columbia House Company. (1992). Spies: Spying for the KGB. [Motion Picture]. (Available from: Columbia House Video Library, 1400 North Fruitage Avenue, Terre Haute, IN, 47811)

The Columbia House Company. (1992). Spies: Traitors. [Motion Picture]. (Available from: Columbia House Video Library, 1400 North Fruitage Avenue, Terre Haute, IN, 47811)

The Columbia House Company. (1992). Spies: Undercover Spies. [Motion Picture]. (Available from: Columbia House Video Library, 1400 North Fruitage Avenue, Terre Haute, IN, 47811)

The Columbia House Company. (1992). Spies: Wartime Espionage. [Motion Picture]. (Available from: Columbia House Video Library, 1400 North Fruitage Avenue, Terre Haute, IN, 47811)

The Editors of Sports Illustrated. (1993). The Sports Illustrated 1993 Sports Almanac. New York: Bishop Books. ISBN: 0-316-80810-5.

The Editors of The Wall Street Journal. (1989). The Wall Street Journal. Book of Chief Executive Style. New York: William Morrow and Company Inc. ISBN: 0-688-07922-9.

The Editors of Time-Life Books, with a foreword by Capps, B. (1973). The Old West: Indians. New York: Time-Life Books. Library of Congress Catalog Card Number: 72-93991.

The Editors of Time-Life Books, with a foreword by Capps, B. (1975). The Old West: The Great Chiefs. Alexandria, VA. Time-Life Books. Library of Congress Catalog Card Number: 75-744.

The Editors of Time-Life Books, with a foreword by Forbis, W. (1973). The Old West: The Cowboys. New York: Time-Life Books. Library of Congress Catalog Card Number: 72-87680.

The Editors of Time-Life Books, with a foreword by Trachtman, P. (1974). The Old West: The Gunfighters. Alexandria, VA: Time-Life Books. Library of Congress Catalog Card Number: 74-80284.

The History Channel. (1996). 20th Century with Mike Wallace: Guns & God; The Sieges of Waco & Ruby Ridge. [Motion Picture]. (Available from New Group Video, 126 Fifth Avenue, New York, NY 10011)

The History Channel. (1996). <u>20th Century with Mike Wallace: Terror Strikes Home, The World Trade Center Bombing.</u> [Motion Picture]. (Available from New Video Group, 126 Fifth Avenue, New York, NY 10011)

The History Channel. (1996). <u>History's Mysteries: Contaminated, The Karen Silkwood Story.</u> [Motion Picture]. (Available from New Video Group, 126 Fifth Avenue, New York, NY 10011)

<u>The Holy Bible.</u> (1973). Hazelwood, MO: Word AFlame Press.

<u>The Holy Bible.</u> (1984). Serendipity New Testament for Groups (2nd ed.). Littleton, CO: Serendipity House.

<u>The Holy Bible.</u> (1985). Nashville, TN: National Publishing Company.

<u>The Illustrated Science and Invention Encyclopedia.</u> (International ed., Vol. 1). (1974). Westport, CT: H.S. Stuttman, Inc.

<u>The Illustrated Science and Invention Encyclopedia.</u> (International ed., Vol. 2). (1974). Westport, CT: H.S. Stuttman, Inc.

<u>The Illustrated Science and Invention Encyclopedia.</u> (International ed., Vol. 3). (1974). Westport, CT: H.S. Stuttman, Inc.

<u>The Illustrated Science and Invention Encyclopedia.</u> (International ed., Vol. 4). (1974). Westport, CT: H.S. Stuttman, Inc.

<u>The Illustrated Science and Invention Encyclopedia.</u> (International ed., Vol. 5). (1974). Westport, CT: H.S. Stuttman, Inc.

<u>The Illustrated Science and Invention Encyclopedia.</u> (International ed., Vol. 6). (1974). Westport, CT: H.S. Stuttman, Inc.

<u>The Illustrated Science and Invention Encyclopedia.</u> (International ed., Vol. 7). (1974). Westport, CT: H.S. Stuttman, Inc.

<u>The Illustrated Science and Invention Encyclopedia.</u> (International ed., Vol. 8). (1974). Westport, CT: H.S. Stuttman, Inc.

<u>The Illustrated Science and Invention Encyclopedia.</u> (International ed., Vol. 9). (1974). Westport, CT: H.S. Stuttman, Inc.

<u>The Illustrated Science and Invention Encyclopedia.</u> (International ed., Vol. 10). (1974). Westport, CT: H.S. Stuttman, Inc.

<u>The Illustrated Science and Invention Encyclopedia.</u> (International ed., Vol. 11). (1974). Westport, CT: H.S. Stuttman, Inc.

<u>The Illustrated Science and Invention Encyclopedia.</u> (International ed., Vol. 12). (1974). Westport, CT: H.S. Stuttman, Inc.

<u>The Illustrated Science and Invention Encyclopedia.</u> (International ed., Vol. 13). (1974). Westport, CT: H.S. Stuttman, Inc.

<u>The Illustrated Science and Invention Encyclopedia.</u> (International ed., Vol. 14). (1974). Westport, CT: H.S. Stuttman, Inc.

<u>The Illustrated Science and Invention Encyclopedia.</u> (International ed., Vol. 15). (1974). Westport, CT: H.S. Stuttman, Inc.

The Illustrated Science and Invention Encyclopedia. (International ed., Vol. 16). (1974). Westport, CT: H.S. Stuttman, Inc.
The Illustrated Science and Invention Encyclopedia. (International ed., Vol. 17). (1974). Westport, CT: H.S. Stuttman, Inc.
The Illustrated Science and Invention Encyclopedia. (International ed., Vol. 18). (1974). Westport, CT: H.S. Stuttman, Inc.
The Illustrated Science and Invention Encyclopedia. (International ed., Vol. 19). (1974). Westport, CT: H.S. Stuttman, Inc.
The Illustrated Science and Invention Encyclopedia. (International ed., Vol. 20). (1974). Westport, CT: H.S. Stuttman, Inc.
The Illustrated Science and Invention Encyclopedia. (International ed., Vol. 21). (1974). Westport, CT: H.S. Stuttman, Inc.
The Illustrated Science and Invention Encyclopedia. (International ed., Vol. 22). (1974). Westport, CT: H.S. Stuttman, Inc.
The Illustrated Science and Invention Encyclopedia. (International ed., Vol. 23). (1974). Westport, CT: H.S. Stuttman, Inc.
The Library of Congress. (1995). Historic Presidential Speeches: Volume 1: William Taft, Theodore Roosevelt, Woodrow Wilson, Warren G. Harding, Calvin Coolidge, and Herbert Hoover. (Cassette Recording). Los Angeles, CA: Rhino Records, Inc.
The Library of Congress. (1995). Historic Presidential Speeches: Volume 2: Franklin D. Roosevelt and Harry S. Truman. (Cassette Recording). Los Angeles, CA: Rhino Records, Inc.
The Library of Congress. (1995). Historic Presidential Speeches: Volume 3: Dwight D. Eisenhower, John F. Kennedy, and Lyndon B. Johnson. (Cassette Recording). Los Angeles, CA: Rhino Records, Inc.
The Library of Congress. (1995). Historic Presidential Speeches: Volume 4: Richard Nixon, Gerald Ford, and Jimmy Carter. (Cassette Recording). Los Angeles, CA: Rhino Records, Inc.
The Library of Congress. (1995). Historic Presidential Speeches: Volume 5: Ronald Reagan and George Bush. (Cassette Recording). Los Angeles, CA: Rhino Records, Inc.
The Library of Congress. (1995). Historic Presidential Speeches: Volume 6: William J. Clinton. (Cassette Recording). Los Angeles, CA: Rhino Records, Inc.
The New Testament. (1971). Good News for Modern Man: The New Testament in Today's English Version (3rd ed.). Hawthorne, NJ: The Free Bible Literature Society.
The Ohio Oil Company. (1950-1961). Employee Booklets. Findlay, OH: The Ohio Oil Company.

The Old Testament of the New American Bible. (Cassette Recording, Tape 13, Vol. 1). (1991). Washington, D.C.: Confraternity of Christian Doctrine.
The Old Testament of the New American Bible. (Cassette Recording, Tape 14, Vol. 1). (1991). Washington, D.C.: Confraternity of Christian Doctrine.
The Old Testament of the New American Bible. (Cassette Recording, Tape 15, Vol. 1). (1991). Washington, D.C.: Confraternity of Christian Doctrine.
The Old Testament of the New American Bible. (Cassette Recording, Tape 16, Vol. 1). (1991). Washington, D.C.: Confraternity of Christian Doctrine.
The Old Testament of the New American Bible. (Cassette Recording, Tape 17, Vol. 1). (1991). Washington, D.C.: Confraternity of Christian Doctrine.
The Old Testament of the New American Bible. (Cassette Recording, Tape 18, Vol. 1). (1991). Washington, D.C.: Confraternity of Christian Doctrine.
The Old Testament of the New American Bible. (Cassette Recording, Tape 19, Vol. 1). (1991). Washington, D.C.: Confraternity of Christian Doctrine.
The Old Testament of the New American Bible. (Cassette Recording, Tape 20, Vol. 1). (1991). Washington, D.C.: Confraternity of Christian Doctrine.
The Old Testament of the New American Bible. (Cassette Recording, Tape 21, Vol. 1). (1991). Washington, D.C.: Confraternity of Christian Doctrine.
The Old Testament of the New American Bible. (Cassette Recording, Tape 22, Vol. 1). (1991). Washington, D.C.: Confraternity of Christian Doctrine.
The Old Testament of the New American Bible. (Cassette Recording, Tape 23, Vol. 1). (1991). Washington, D.C.: Confraternity of Christian Doctrine.
The Old Testament of the New American Bible. (Cassette Recording, Tape 24, Vol. 1). (1991). Washington, D.C.: Confraternity of Christian Doctrine.
The Old Testament of the New American Bible. (Cassette Recording, Tape 25, Vol. 2). (1991). Washington, D.C.: Confraternity of Christian Doctrine.
The Old Testament of the New American Bible. (Cassette Recording, Tape 26, Vol. 2). (1991). Washington, D.C.: Confraternity of Christian Doctrine.
The Old Testament of the New American Bible. (Cassette Recording, Tape 27, Vol. 2). (1991). Washington, D.C.: Confraternity of Christian Doctrine.
The Old Testament of the New American Bible. (Cassette Recording, Tape 28, Vol. 2). (1991). Washington, D.C.: Confraternity of Christian Doctrine.
The Old Testament of the New American Bible. (Cassette Recording, Tape 29, Vol. 2). (1991). Washington, D.C.: Confraternity of Christian Doctrine.
The Old Testament of the New American Bible. (Cassette Recording, Tape 30, Vol. 2). (1991). Washington, D.C.: Confraternity of Christian Doctrine.
The Old Testament of the New American Bible. (Cassette Recording, Tape 31, Vol. 2). (1991). Washington, D.C.: Confraternity of Christian Doctrine.
The Old Testament of the New American Bible. (Cassette Recording, Tape 32, Vol. 2). (1991). Washington, D.C.: Confraternity of Christian Doctrine.

The Old Testament of the New American Bible. (Cassette Recording, Tape 33, Vol. 2). (1991). Washington, D.C.: Confraternity of Christian Doctrine.
The Old Testament of the New American Bible. (Cassette Recording, Tape 34, Vol. 2). (1991). Washington, D.C.: Confraternity of Christian Doctrine.
The Old Testament of the New American Bible. (Cassette Recording, Tape 35, Vol. 2). (1991). Washington, D.C.: Confraternity of Christian Doctrine.
The Old Testament of the New American Bible. (Cassette Recording, Tape 36, Vol. 2). (1991). Washington, D.C.: Confraternity of Christian Doctrine.
The Old Testament of the New American Bible. (Cassette Recording, Tape 44, Vol. 3). (1991). Washington, D.C.: Confraternity of Christian Doctrine.
The Old Testament of the New American Bible. (Cassette Recording, Tape 45, Vol. 3). (1991). Washington, D.C.: Confraternity of Christian Doctrine.
The Old Testament of the New American Bible. (Cassette Recording, Tape 46, Vol. 3). (1991). Washington, D.C.: Confraternity of Christian Doctrine.
The Old Testament of the New American Bible. (Cassette Recording, Tape 47, Vol. 3). (1991). Washington, D.C.: Confraternity of Christian Doctrine.
The Old Testament of the New American Bible. (Cassette Recording, Tape 48, Vol. 3). (1991). Washington, D.C.: Confraternity of Christian Doctrine.
The Old Testament of the New American Bible. (Cassette Recording, Tape 49, Vol. 3). (1991). Washington, D.C.: Confraternity of Christian Doctrine.
The Old Testament of the New American Bible. (Cassette Recording, Tape 50, Vol. 3). (1991). Washington, D.C.: Confraternity of Christian Doctrine.
The Old Testament of the New American Bible. (Cassette Recording, Tape 51, Vol. 3). (1991). Washington, D.C.: Confraternity of Christian Doctrine.
The Old Testament of the New American Bible. (Cassette Recording, Tape 52, Vol. 3). (1991). Washington, D.C.: Confraternity of Christian Doctrine.
The Old Testament of the New American Bible. (Cassette Recording, Tape 53, Vol. 3). (1991). Washington, D.C.: Confraternity of Christian Doctrine.
The Old Testament of the New American Bible. (Cassette Recording, Tape 54, Vol. 3). (1991). Washington, D.C.: Confraternity of Christian Doctrine.
The Old Testament of the New American Bible.(Cassette Recording, Tape 43, Vol. 3). (1991). Washington, D.C.: Confraternity of Christian Doctrine.
The Options Industry Council (Writers). (1993). The Options Tool. [Motion Picture]. United States: The Options Industry Council.
The Reader's Digest, Wernert, S. (Ed.). (1982). North American Wildlife. Pleasantville, NY: The Reader's Digest Association, Inc. ISBN: 0-89577-102-0.
The Reader's Digest. (1975). The Story of America. Pleasantville, NY: The Reader's Digest Association, Inc. Library of Congress Catalog Card Number: 75-3837.

The Reader's Digest. (1977). Fix-it-Yourself Manual. Pleasantville, NY: The Reader's Digest Association, Inc. ISBN: 0-89577-040-7.

The Reader's Digest. (1991). Today's Best Nonfiction. Pleasantville, NY: The Reader's Digest Association, Inc. ISSN: 0893-9373.

The Reader's Digest. (1996). Reader's Digest Condensed Books. Pleasantville, NY: The Reader's Digest Association, Inc. Library of Congress Catalog Card Number: 50-12721.

The Staff of the Wall Street Journal. (1998). The Wall Street Journal Almanac. 1999. New York: Ballantine Books. ISBN: 0-345-41102-1.

Thomas, G., & Finney, R. (1992). Calculus and Analytic Geometry (8th ed.). Reading, MA: Addison-Wesley Publishing Company. ISBN: 0-201-53286-7.

Thomas, G., & Morgan-Witts, M. (1979). The Day the Bubble Burst: The Social History of the Wall Street Crash of 1929. Dallas, PA: Penguin Books. ISBN: 0-14-00-5640-8.

Thompson, A., & Formby, J. (1993). Economics of the Firm: Theory and Practice (6th ed.). Englewood Cliffs, NJ: Prentice-Hall, Inc. ISBN: 0-13-092867-4.

Thoreau, H.D. (1993). Civil Disobedience and Other Essays. Toronto, Ontario: Dover Thrift Editions. ISBN: 0-486-27563-9.

Thurow, L. (1983). Dangerous Currents: The State of Economics. New York: Vintage Books. ISBN:0-394-72368-6.

Thurow, L. (1992). Head to Head: The Coming Economic Battle among Japan, Europe, and America. New York, NY: William Morrow and Company, Inc. ISBN: 0-688-11150-5.

Thurow, L. (1999). Building Wealth: The New Rules for Individuals, Companies, and Nations in a Knowledge-Based Economy. New York: HarperCollins Publishers. ISBN: 0-88730-951-8.

Thurow, L.C. (1996). The Future of Capitalism: How Today's Economic Forces Shape Tomorrow's World. New York, NY: Penguin Books. ISBN: 0-14-026328-4.

Tietenberg, T. (1998). Environmental Economics and Policy (2nd ed.). Reading, MA: Addison-Wesley. ISBN: 0-321-01142-2.

Tiper, P. (982). Physics (2nd ed.). New York: Worth Publishers, Inc. ISBN: 0-87901-135-1.

Tipler, P. (1978). Modern Physics. New York: Worth Publishers, Inc. ISBN: 0-87901-088-6.

Toffler, A. (1980). The Third Wave. New York: Bantam Books. ISBN: 0-553-24698-4.

Toffler, A. (Speaker) (1990). Power Shift. (Cassette Recording). New York: Bantam Audio Publishing. ISBN: 0-553-45263-0.

Toffler, A., & Toffler, H. with foreword by Gingrich, N. (1994, 1995). Creating a New Civilization: The Politics of the Third Wave. Atlanta, GA: Turner Publishing, Inc. ISBN: 1-57036-224-6.

Tofler, A. (1970). Future Shock. New York: Bantam Books.

Tofler, A. (1990). Power Shift: Knowledge, Wealth, and Violence at the Edge of the 21st Century. New York, NY: Bantam Books. ISBN: 0-553-29215-3.

Tolstoy, L. (1992). War and Peace. New York: Barnes & Noble Classics. ISBN: 1-56619-27-4.

Trout, M. (Speaker) (1995). Life on the Edge, by Dr. James Dobson. (Cassette Recording). Dallas, TX: Word Publishing. ISBN: 0-8799-6059-2.

Twain, M. (1920). The Adventures of Tom Sawyer. New York: Bantam Books. ISBN: 0-553-2101-7.

Twain, M. (1988). The Adventures of Huckleberry Finn. New York: Bantam Books. ISBN: 0-553-21079-3.

Tzu, S. (1996). The Art of War. West Hollywood, CA: Dove Books. ISBN: 0-7871-0561.

U.S. Geological Survey. (Unknown). Ariel Photographs and Satellite Images. Unknown: U.S. Department of the Interior.

Underwood, R.S., & Sparks, F.W. (1948). Analytic Geometry. Cambridge, MA: Houghton Mifflin Company.

Uris, L. (1963). Armageddon. New York: Dell. ISBN: 0-440-10290-1.

Valauskas, E.J., & Ertel, M. (1996). The Internet for Teachers and School Library Media Specialists: Today's applications tomorrows prospects. New York, NY: Neal-Schuman Publishers, Inc.

Valkenburg, M.E. (1982). Analog Filter Design. New York: Holt, Rinehart and Winston. ISBN: 0-03-059246-1.

Van De Graff, K.M. (1992). Human Anatomy (3rd ed.). Dubuque, IA: Wm. C. Brown Publishers. ISBN: 0-697-7892-2.

Van Horne, J. (1983). Financial Management and Policy (6th ed.). Englewood Cliffs, NJ: Prentice Hall. ISBN: 0-13-316026-2.

Varian, H. (1987). Intermediate Microeconomics: A Modern Approach. New York: W.W. Norton & Company, Inc. ISBN: 0-393-95554-0.

Varian, H. (1992). Microeconomic Analysis (3rd ed.). New York: W.W. Norton & Company, Inc. ISBN: 0-393-95735-7.

Varian, H. (1993). Intermediate Microeconomics: A Modern Approach (3rd ed.). New York: W.W. Norton & Company, Inc. ISBN: 0-393-96320-9.

Various Authors. (1941). World's Greatest Books. New York: WM. H. Wise & Co.

Various-Barker, S., Lagerkvist, P., Beaton, C., Seton, C., Andrews, C., Durrell, G., Kelly, W., & James, H. (1954). Fire and the Hammer; Barabbas; an excerpt from The Glass of Fashion; an excerpt from Helen Gould Was My

Mother-In-Law; an excerpt from The Overloaded Ark; a photo feature, Voyages and Discoveries; an excerpt from I Go Pogo; and Washington Square. New York: Best in Books/Nelson Doubleday, Inc.

Various-Keyes, F., Runyon, M., Bergane, V., Tilden, F., Daphne du Maurier, Barkley, A., Costain, T., Goldberg, R., Boal, S., & Bombard, Dr. A. (1954). The Royal Box; a photo feature, Our National Parks; Jamaica Inn; an excerpt from That Reminds Me; an excerpt from The White and Gold; a cartoon feature Rube Goldberg's Guide to Europe; and an excerpt from The Voyage of the Heretique. New York: Best in Books/Nelson Doubleday, Inc.

Various-Lofts, N., Chamberlain, A., Rich, L., Kane, H., Runyon, A.M., Bergane, V., O'Malley, B., & Andrews, R. (1955). Eleanor the Queen; The Tall Dark Man; an excerpt from Innocence Under the Elms; an excerpt from Spies for the Blue and Gray; photos entitled Switzerland; a cartoon feature Blessed Event, and an excerpt from Trails of the World. New York: Best in Books/Nelson Doubleday, Inc.

Various-Michener, J., Collins, A., Rinehart, M., Daphne du Maurier, Sixta, Cronin, A.J., Dumas, F., & Cousteau, J.Y. (unknown publishing date). The Bridges at Toko-Ri; The Story of Aviation; The Swimming Pool; Kiss Me Again, Stranger; Rivets; Adventures in Two Worlds; The Silent World; and Short Stories Do De Maupassant. New York: Best in Books/Nelson Doubleday, Inc.

Veblen, T. (1919). The Vested Interests and the Common Man. New York: Sentry Press. Library of Congress Catalogue Card Number: 63-23513.

Veblen, T. with an introduction by Berg, I. (1993). The Higher Learning in America. New Brunswick, NJ: Transaction. ISBN: 1-56000-600-5.

Veblen, T. with an introduction by Dowd, D. (1978). The Theory of Business Enterprise. New Brunswick, NJ: Transaction Publishers. ISBN: 0-87855-699-0.

Veblen, T. with an introduction by Levy, M. Jr. (1997). Absentee Ownership: Business Enterprise in Recent Times: The Case of America. New Brunswick, NJ: Transaction. ISBN: 1-56000-922-5.

Veblen, T. with an introduction by Murphey, M. (1990). The Instinct of Workmanship and the State of the Industrial Arts. New Brunswick, NJ: Transaction. ISBN: 0-88738-807-8.

Veblen, T. with an introduction by Samuels, W. (1998). The Nature of Peace. New Brunswick, NJ: Transaction. ISBN: 1-56000-973-X.

Veblin, T. (1998, originally 1899). Theory of the Leisure Class. Amherst, NY: Prometheus Books Great Minds Series.

Ventura, J. (1999). I Ain't Got Time to Bleed: Reworking the Body Politic from the Bottom Up. New York: Villard Books. ISBN: 0-375-50332-3.

Vermes, G. (1962). The Dead Sea Scrolls in English. London, England: Penguin Books.

Vernon, W. (1976). Introductory Psychology: A Personalized Textbook (2nd ed., Rev.). Chicago, IL: Rand McNally & Company. Library of Congress Catalog Card Number: 75-16807.

VocabuLearn. (1986). VocabuLearn Spanish. (Cassette Recording). Carlsbad, CA: Penton Overseas, Inc. ISBN: 0-939001-10-1.

Wagnleitner, R., & May, E.T. (2000). Here, There and Everywhere: The Foreign Politics of American Popular Culture. Hanover, NH: University Press of New England. ISBN: 1-58465-035-4.

Waldrop, M.M. (1992). Complexity: The Emerging Science at the Edge of Order and Chaos. New York, NY: Touchstone. ISBN: 0-671-87234-6.

Warmington, E., & Rouse, P. (Eds.). (1984). Great Dialogues of Plato. New York: A Mentor Book. Library of Congress Catalog Card Number: 56-7927.

Warrilow, D. (Speaker) (1989). The Art of War, by Sun Tzu. Translated by Thomas Cleary. (Cassette Recording). Boston, MA: Shambhala Publications, Inc. ISBN: 0-87773-515-8.

Washington, B.T. (1955). Up From Slavery. New York, NY: Dover Publications, Inc. ISBN: 0-486-28738-6.

Watkins, T.H. (1993). The Great Depression: America in the 1930's. Boston, MA: Little, Brown and Company. ISBN: 0-316-92453-9.

Watson, T., & Petre, P. (1990). Father Son & Co.: My Life at IBM and Beyond. New York: Bantam Books. ISBN: 0-553-07011-8.

Watts, R. (1977). Our Freedom Documents (Rev. ed.). Washington, D.C.: The Supreme Council.

Weast, R.C. (Ed.). (1985). CRC Handbook of Chemistry and Physics (66th ed.). Boca Raton, FL: CRC Press, Inc. ISBN: 0-8493-0466-0.

Weber, M. (1930). The Protestant Ethic and the Spirit of Capitalism. London, England: Routledge. ISBN: 0-415-08434-2.

Weber, M. (1978). Economy and Society: An Outline of Interpretive Sociology Vol. I & II. Eds. Guenther Roth, Claus Wittich. California: University of California Press.

Wechsler, D. (1955). WAIS Manual: Wechsler Adult Intelligence Scale. New York: The Psychological Corporation.

Wellman, F. (1936). The Art of Cross-Examination (4th ed.). New York: Macmillan Publishing Company. ISBN: 0-02-071960-0.

Whaples, R., & Mason, C. (1999). Study Guide to accompany Microeconomics. Reading, MA: Addison Wesley Longman, Inc. ISBN: 0-201-3809-2.

Whittemore, H. (1990). <u>CNN The Inside Story: How a Band of Mavericks Changed the Face of Television News.</u> Boston, MA: Little, Brown and Company. ISBN: 0-316-93761-4.

Wicker, T. (1991). <u>One of Us: Richard Nixon and The American Dream.</u> New York: Random House. ISBN: 0-394-55066-8.

Wilkie, B., & Hurt, J. (1992). <u>Literature of the Western World: Neoclassicism Through the Modern Period</u> (Vol. 2, 3rd ed.). New York: Macmillan Publishing Company. ISBN: 0-02-427827-0.

Willams, H. (1988). <u>Study Guide: Peterson's Income, Employment, & Economic Growth</u> (6th ed.). New York: W.W. Norton & Company. ISBN: 0-393-95631-8.

Williams, J., Metcalfe, H.C., Trinklein, F., & Lefler, R. (1968). <u>Modern Physics.</u> New York: Holt, Rinehart and Winston, Inc. ISBN: 03-063540-3.

Willmington, H.L. (1987). <u>Book of Bible Lists.</u> Wheaton, IL: Tyndale House Publishers, Inc. ISBN: 0-8423-8803-6.

Wills, G. (Ed.). (1982). <u>The Federalist Papers by Alexander Hamilton, James Madison, and John Jay.</u> New York: Bantam Books. ISBN: 0-553-21340-7.

Wilson, J. (1980). <u>American Government: Institutions and Policies.</u> Lexington, MA: D.C. Heath and Company. ISBN: 0-669-04560-8.

Wilson, R. (1991). <u>Conducting Better Interviews.</u> New York: Barron's Educational Series, Inc. ISBN: 0-8120-4580-7.

Wise, G. (1979). <u>Some Elementary Axioms for an American Cultural Studies.</u> Prospects 4. Pp. 517-47.

Wister, O. (1992). <u>The Virginian: A Horseman of the Plains.</u> Lincoln, NE: University of Nebraska Press. ISBN: 0-8032-9736-X.

Wister, O. (1993). <u>The Virginian.</u> Los Angeles, CA: The Publishing Mills-Audio Books. ISBN: 1-879371-48-0.

Wonnacott, P., & Wonnacott, R. (1990). <u>Test Bank: Economics</u> (4th ed.). New York: John Wiley & Sons, Inc. ISBN: 0-471-51618-X.

Woodward, B. (1987). <u>Veil: The Secret Wars of the CIA 1981-1987.</u> New York: Simon & Schuster. ISBN: 0-671-60117-2.

Woodworth, J. (1919). <u>Hardening, Tempering, Annealing, and Forging of Steel.</u> (5th ed.). New York: The Norman W. Henley Publishing Company.

World Bank. (2000). <u>Entering the 21st Century: World Development Report 1999/2000.</u> New York, NY: Oxford University Press, Inc. ISBN: 0-19-521124-3.

Worster, D. (1994). <u>Nature's Economy: A History of Ecological Ideas.</u> New York, NY: Cambridge University Press. ISBN: 0-521-46834-5.

Wright, P. (1987). <u>Spy Catcher.</u> New York: Dell Publishing. ISBN: 0-440-20132-2.

Wright, W. (1975). Sixguns and Society: A Structural Study of the Western. Berkeley: University of California Press.
Wyoming Game and Fish Department. (1976). Considerations for Wildlife in Industrial Development and Reclamation. Cheyenne, WY: Wyoming Game and Fish Department.
Wyoming Game and Fish Department. (1985). The Mule Deer of Wyoming (2nd ed.). Cheyenne, WY: Wyoming Game and Fish Department.
Xenophon. (1997). Memorabilia Oeconomicus. Eds. G.P. Goold. London, England: Harvard University Press. ISBN: 0-674-99186-9.
Yeoman, R.S. (1993). A Guide Book of United States Coins (47th ed.). Racine, WI: Western Publishing Company. ISBN: 0-307-19887-1.
Yergin, D. (1991). The Prize: The Epic Quest for Oil, Money, & Power. New York: Simon & Schuster. ISBN: 0-671-79932-0.
Yergin, D. (1997). Shattered Peace: The Origins of the Cold War. New York: The Penguin Group. ISBN: 0 14 01.2177-3.
Yergin, D., & Gustafson, T. (1993). Russia 2010 and What it Means for the World. New York: Vintage Books, A Division of Random House, Inc. ISBN: 0-679-42995-6.
Yergin, D., & Stanislaw, J. (1998). The Commanding Heights: The Battle Between Government and the Marketplace that is Remaking the Modern World. New York: Simon & Schuster. ISBN: 0-684-82975-4.
Young, J. (1981). Illustrated Encyclopedic Dictionary of Electronics. West Nyack, NY: Parker Publishing Company, Inc. ISBN: 0-13-450791-6.
Yourdon, E. (1993). Decline & Fall of the American Programmer. Englewood Cliffs, NJ: Yourdon Press. ISBN: 0-13-191958-X.
Yudkin, M. (1988). Freelance Writing for Magazines and Newspapers: Breaking In Without Selling Out. New York: Harper & Row. ISBN: 0-06-055134-8.
Zera'im, S. (1948). The Babylonian Talmud. Eds. Rabbi Dr. I. Epstein. Netherlands: The Soncino Press of London. Coe Call #: BM 500.2 E57 v. 14.
Zitarelli, D., & Coughlin, R. (1992). Finite Mathematics with Calculus: An Applied Approach (2nd ed.). Fort Worth, TX: Saunders College Publishing. ISBN: 0-03-055849-2.
Zitarelli, D., & Coughlin, R. (1992). Finite Mathematics with Calculus: An Applied Approach (2nd ed.). Fort Worth, TX: Saunders College Publishing. ISBN: 0-03-055849-2.
Zupnick, E. (1999). Visions and Revisions: The United States in the Global Economy. Boulder, CO: Westview Press, a Member of the Perseus Books Group. ISBN: 0-8133-3552-3.
Zygmunt, J. (1992). Environmental Law and Policy: Nature, Law, and Society. St. Paul, MN: West Publishing Company. 0-314-00341-X.

If you need to type anything after the reference list then start it on this page

INDEX

American Studies, 3, 23, 39, 50, 60, 67, 103, 112-113, 122, 128

Bacon-Smith, Camille, 1

Basketball event, 4, 7-21, 23-25, 27, 29-34, 38-48

    6th Man Club, 3, 6-9, 14, 21, 23, 36, 45, 55

    Advertising, 5, 14, 20, 25, 38, 45-48, 106

    Arena-Auditorium (AA) or 'double-A, viii, 4, 9, 12, 19

    Beer Song, 24, 56

    Cotton-Eyed Joe, 9, 19, 24, 40-42, 56

    Cowboy Joe Club, 4-8, 11-15, 19, 22, 30-31, 33, 35, 46, 55

    Game
        Audio, 3, 13, 17, 35-36, 45, 67, 72, 79, 98, 100, 106, 109, 112, 116-117, 128-129, 136
        Pre-Game, 17, 45
        First-Half, 20
        Halftime, 6, 16, 21-23, 29, 40, 60, 127
        Second-Half, 23
        Post-Game, 26-27
        Practice, 9, 16, 27-29, 40, 70, 72, 77, 91, 98-99, 104, 136
            Suicides, 28

Narrative Structure or sequence of the basketball event, 40

NCAA 1943 Championship video clip, 4, 8, 15

Obscenities, 4, 42, 44

Papa John's Pizza Scream, 21, 42

Rabid fans, 1, 4, 11, 13, 23, 29, 41, 43-44, 47

Ragtime Cowboy Joe, 18, 36, 40, 61

Audio, 3, 13, 17, 35-36, 45, 67, 72, 79, 98, 100, 106, 109, 112, 116-117, 128-129, 136

Relative Loudness Levels or Hierarchy of Event Moments, 42

Ticket Brochure(s) & schedule & AA Seating Chart, 53

Wildfire, 8, 18, 20, 22, 36

Cheering for self, 1, 10, 12, 14, 16-17, 23, 27, 32-34, 39-45, 47-48

Dorst, John, 59, 84

Feinstein, John, 6, 37, 49

History, UW Basketball, 7

Leach, Eugene, 60

Levi-Strauss, Claude, 47

Participant observation mini-ethnography, 2, 9

Sandeen, Eric, 3

0-595-27980-5